LIVE IT
love it
SELL IT

LIVE IT love it SELL IT

How to win at sales with the art of human conversation

Jules White

CAVALCADE BOOKS

Live It, Love It, Sell It®

First published in the United Kingdom in 2018
by Cavalcade Books
www.cavalcadebooks.com

ISBN 978-1-9996213-2-2

Cover design by Colourburst Lithographic Ltd

Contents

Foreword by Eleanor Goold

I simply couldn't watch any longer.

I pulled the cushion up in front of my face, and tentatively peeked over when I thought it might be safe again.

Only to find my worst nightmare playing out right before my eyes.

There were sweaty palms, terrified looks ...and, in some cases, complete stage fright paralysis!

There was absolutely nowhere to hide.

And I was only watching a television programme!

It seems silly now, but back when I first saw it BBC's hit TV show *Dragons' Den* showed me the stuff of my nightmares. I would rather have been a contestant on *Masterchef* (and I'm a terrible cook by the way) or be dunked in gunge, than have had anything to do with that awful S word ...sales, let alone what the contestants on *Dragons' Den* were doing.

I don't know where this aversion stemmed from, but any activity where I had to talk and sell myself I found utterly excruciating. Job interviews, in particular, would terrify me more than anything else.

Whenever I was asked to do any form of pitch, I would freeze, get my words all muddled up (which for a writer is inexcusable) and generally make a fool of myself.

I had it indelibly etched in my mind – sales is a very bad word.

And as for salespeople ...ewwww ...no thanks.

The ones I encountered were generally pushy in their approach and more concerned about hitting their targets than ever caring about the consumer's needs.

My one experience of ever actually selling anything only lasted one day. It was a job in telesales, and I got sacked for 'time wasting' following what I thought was a pleasant conversation with a 'hot lead'.

If only I'd known…

Fast forward a few years later when I finally ventured out and started my own copywriting company. 'Sweet talking sales in print' suited me. I definitely had a way with words, but I was still self-conscious about actually selling my services in person.

I still had the niggling voice in the back of my head: 'You may be good on paper, but when it comes down to it you can't sell in person!'

All that changed when I met Jules. A real-life dragon slayer who had been on *Dragons' Den*, and won!

She was nothing like the idea I had in my head of a salesperson. She was completely the opposite, in fact. She had a really lovely energy about her, authentic in every way, someone who simply wanted to help people. Gosh! What's that all about I thought to myself?

I decided to find out.

I joined one of her fun Facebook challenges – this one was about learning how to pitch. Me, pitching? As it turned out I wasn't as bad as I thought I'd be and was overjoyed to come in second place and win a breakthrough call with Jules.

We hit it off straight away and what she taught me in that short hour changed my life and has helped me ever since.

It just seemed so natural.

I was hooked with this new art of sales, which turned out to be the art of good conversation – in your language, to the people who like and are attracted to you.

Who knew!

In this inspiring book, Jules takes you on a voyage of personal discovery where you will realise that sales doesn't have to be difficult, stressful or appear needy and desperate.

In fact, it is quite the opposite. It can be fun, hugely rewarding and benefit everyone.

When it comes to pitching and sales, I no longer put the metaphorical cushion in front of my face and dread what's coming next.

Instead, thanks to Jules, given the chance I am now the first person to jump centre stage and set about doing my own unique 'pitch' performance, bellowing proudly at the top of my voice and enjoying every minute of it.

'Live It, Love It, Sell It' was definitely a game changer for me.

Once you have read this book, you too will be shining in your own spotlight and savouring every magical moment.

This is more than a book; it's a guide brimming full of wisdom that you can dip into again and again …in fact, I am going to do that right now.

Because as Jules likes to say: there's no such word as can't.

Thank you, Jules, for showing us the way.

The Aggressive Sales King is Dead, Long Live the Queen of Authentic Selling!

Eleanor Goold, August 2018

Founder and Creative Director, Kreativ Copywriting
Podcast co-host of 'The Anti-Social Chat Show'
Creator of the Utterly Compelling series of online content and copywriting courses

Acknowledgements

The hardest part of writing these acknowledgements is knowing where to start. So many people have helped me, not just in bringing this book to print but in my journey to the point where I was ready to write it. So, with apologies to anyone I've forgotten, here goes.

First, I want to thank my dear mum and dad. They are no longer on this Earth, but they walk every step with me through my life, holding my hand. They gave me amazing foundations for my life. My dad continually told me, 'There is no such word as can't,' and I've carried that lesson with me all through my life.

Thanks go to the school friends who are still my cheerleaders, even from afar: Lynn Curran; Elaine Grix, an amazing coach herself who gave me the belief that I could be a coach; Paul Metrovich, who has believed in me since we were five years old; and Andy Fish, who is actually so scared I will beat him at golf that he still hasn't organised that game!

And to the people who have helped me in my sales career: the great managers who taught me so much, Jon Sillé and Michael Schofield; the brilliant sales colleagues who are still supporting me and who, even though I don't work with them anymore, believe in everything I do, Ellie Wilson and Philip Keech.

From my Truly Madly Baby days, I want to thank Tina Ringsell, who has always remained completely loyal, and the lovely Joanne Barr, who stood by my side when everything else was falling apart.

For helping me to see that I truly had a gift when it came to sales, I'm indebted to my dear friend Irene Crosswell, who we lost far too soon. I know you are walking ahead of me, showing me the way every step I take. And to Ros Ainscow, who has taken over the reins from Irene, and whose support is priceless – I have so much love and respect for you, Ros.

Thanks to my coach Helen Packham, who helped me at the start of my business journey last year. You gave me the clarity I needed.

Every step of your life you meet new people, and I have been so lucky to meet 'my groupies' – an incredible group of people who regularly hang out with me online and continually make me proud with their thirst for knowledge and progression. There are too many names to mention, but they know who they are.

Special thanks go to Karen Ramsay-Smith who wrote about mindful listening for the book – such a wonderful lady. Thank you, Karen, for being you and bringing such great calm energy to my life. To Eleanor who has written the foreword to my book and who has always been a great advocate of my sales methodology - you rock! To my beautiful friend in Jersey Lorraine Pannetier who gave me my beautiful branding colours and has entertained me with many Zoom calls, breakfast on Brighton beach and inspired me with her magical words – she told me I 'sell with soul' and I share this in the book. Thank you Lorraine, you beautiful soul.

Thank you to all my beta readers who have reassured me that this really is a book that will help entrepreneurs and will be their best friend when it comes to sales. The time you have given is really appreciated. It was like waiting for exam results, waiting to hear what you all thought!

This book would also not have been possible without the support of the brilliant Gayle Johnson, who for the last year has read everything I've written towards the book, helped so much with editing and kept me accountable and focused. She truly believed that this book had to be finished and helped me to see it through to completion – an amazing lady.

Thanks too go to my publishers at Cavalcade Books, Suze and Lewis, who have been almost as excited about this book as I am. You two are awesome.

Finally, I have one very important person to thank – my beautiful, funny and clever son Sam. You are my inspiration and my world. I know just how proud you are of me and that makes everything I do worthwhile. Thank you for being you.

Introduction

Live It, Love It, Sell It is for anyone interested in doing sales in a human, non-sleazy, non-pushy way, whether you're male or female, working for yourself or working for an organisation.

If you'd like not just to be able to sell but to fall in love with sales, this book is for you, especially if you are running your own business.

When you have finished reading you will understand that life skills are indeed sales skills. Everyone can sell. You will see that the power lies in:

- using your natural ability
- adjusting your mindset
- developing an understanding of why you do what you do
- tuning into why your ideal client needs your solution

Once you become friends with those four elements, selling will feel as natural as breathing.

My mission in writing this book is to give you the benefit of my experience and knowledge gained from over 30 years of selling. Over that time, I've sold a very diverse range of products, including stainless steel, advertising in Yellow Pages, corporate hospitality, event management, baby products, incentive schemes, recruitment services, software, venue space, exhibition stands and digital marketing. Yes, a long list and huge variety, which of course has taught me a great amount about the art of sales. Everything I have learnt on that journey, every course I've attended, every sale I've made, every team I've led, drives and informs the methodology in this book.

Add to that my successful pitch on *Dragons' Den*, where I won investment from Peter Jones for my business Truly Madly Baby.

This was the business I started when my son Sam was just 3 months old. I had a purpose for doing so, even though most people would say I was mad! I knew the business model I created would help other mums just like me to have a purpose and be able to build their own businesses as well as being mums. I was fiercely ambitious too. I went on to create a globally successful company, but sadly had it all taken away from me. That story will be in my next book!

This book is all about you and all for you. I want you to go out into the world with your fabulous businesses and sell with heart and soul and with no fear. This book will help you to do that.

Live It, Love It, Sell It can't promise that you will be rich – no book can do that – because that is up to you. This book will not tell you that there is only one way to sell, with checklists and magic formulas. If you're used to those sorts of messages, this book should come as a breath of fresh air! It will help you to see that sales is all about connection, relationships and being the true you.

I want this book to hold your hand as a person working in sales or a business owner throughout your journey. I can't order you how to read this book, but it is one that is designed to be read from the beginning to the end, rather than dipped in or out of at first. The exercises too are there to be done, and done in the order in which they're presented. I want you to get the most out of this book and to be sure that you reach the destination on our 'sales road trip' …which is to fall in love with sales.

A very wise man always told me, 'There is no such word as can't.' He was right, and that man was my beautiful dad. And this book will show you that there's no such person as one who can't sell.

LIVE IT

This part of our journey is all about getting fit to travel on the sales road trip. I break this down into the mind, the body and the soul. You will see what I mean as you read on, but fail to start here and it's likely you will not reach the ultimate destination, which is of course the sale.

'One day or day one — you decide.'

Chapter 1

The Mind

Having worked in sales for over 30 years, I've taken part in lots of different sales training courses and worked with many different sales people. All too often, though, I came across the same old messages and theories. And that might be fine if those supposedly key sales ideas were helpful or effective. The problem is they're not!

It's time for us to bust some myths about what sales is and how it works. In this chapter I'm going to address the myths about selling that still do the rounds but are simply not true.

I'm calling this chapter 'The Mind' because it's about the mindset with which we approach selling. There's so much information – and misinformation – that affects how we think about things. And when it comes to selling, some so-called 'facts' can make it seem like it's something not for us or a scary subject. These 'facts' need to be debunked. There's a lot of smoke and mirrors around sales. Let's clear the air straight away.

Exercise

What do you think of when you hear the word 'sales'? Give yourself a minute, take a pen, and write down all the words and feelings you associate with sales and selling.

When you look at the language we hear around sales you may recognise a pattern. For me, for example, when I look at social media and how the 'experts' talk about sales it's all set up as a battle. Here are some of the words I see used, words which I've heard used in the corporate arena for many years and are still used today:

- Push
- Convince
- Targets
- Persuade
- Pressure

If I try and picture the way sales is usually portrayed, I see an arrogant, stressed-out, egotistical con-artist. And I know that's not true! But still, much of the conversation around sales is set out in that tone. The tone that suggests the salesperson is in control and you have to just nod when you're told. Oh, and add to that the idea that you don't know anything about what you really want – they do!

If I think this, then there is a good chance that many others think the same! And that's what causes the negative reactions we have to the mere mention of the word 'sales'.

But this is to look at sales in the wrong light.

I love talking sales with entrepreneurs because it's where sales is the most real, honest and authentic.

Entrepreneurs in small and even medium size businesses are running their businesses based on passion. In many cases, when you ask them they will tell you that passion, challenge or a need has brought them there. Sometimes they have invented something to solve a personal problem they had and it's become a business. Some have left the corporate world because it's not feeding their soul any longer and they want to do something that they find more meaningful or fulfilling. Others again do it for lifestyle reasons, so they can balance work with other passions and commitments. Whatever their reason, entrepreneurs have a great honesty about their businesses and desire to sell in a human way.

For example, one of my amazing clients Chrissie Lowery invented the Cuddle Bed, a fabulous product, which has the most inspiring story behind it. In 2013 she became very unwell very suddenly and she spent nearly a year housebound on the sofa. During this time both of her sons had difficulties at their local village school, and she ended up home-schooling all three of her youngest children whilst trying to get to the bottom of her illness.

She discovered an online community which shared 'life hacks' to support people's health and was inspired by an idea to help her son sleep. Her eldest son's sleep patterns were awful and sometimes he could be awake all night until nearly morning time. He had always been a self-soother and he needed sensory stimulation to help him relax. His bed was always full of toys, pillows and sensory items, so she taught herself to sew and The Cuddle Bed Company was born. She made her son his first 'Snugglebed' and his sleep improved dramatically. Finally, they were not a sleep deprived family, and she also found a purpose and a focus in her life.

Why am I telling you this? Because Chrissie is the direct opposite of being an egotistical con-artist, and she is a highly successful businesswoman. Her product and story are her motivation – her 'why' – and she can sell in a human way where there is no need to push, convince or persuade anyone to buy. She connects with her client, builds a relationship and offers a solution.

Later on, in the **Love It** part of this book, I'll talk about understanding your 'why', finding your ideal client and knowing what their 'why' is. We do this so that we really can sell with integrity and be honest and build trust. The majority of us are not in this to rip people off, push people to buy things they don't need and live a dishonest working life.

If, on the other hand, the methods still being taught out there are adopted, then we run a huge risk of selling in that pushy way – or trying to, then feeling like we've failed at business when it doesn't work.

So, let's look at some of the myths. I could make this list longer or express these myths using other words, but the following five myths capture the key ideas I want to debunk for you, explaining why they're unhelpful or simply wrong.

Sales myth #1: Sales is a numbers game

If I had £1 for every time I heard this…! I bet you've heard it too. In particular, I was told it by bad managers time and time again. I often wondered if it was because they didn't know what else to say. I had one particular manager once who would come out of his office and walk around in silence, observing. (His office was the quietest sales office I had ever worked in – I wonder why?) And he would then announce how much we were missing our targets by. After the announcement he would start walking towards his office, and one day I stopped him and said out loud to the office, 'What would you like us to do, boss?' He replied, 'Sell more,' and went back into his office and shut the door. This was, of course, about the most unhelpful thing he could have said because he was simply stating the obvious. He gave us no direction and the team reverted to trying to hit call numbers and making as many calls as they could every day. Not only was this ineffective as there was no strategy to it, but it was also soul destroying.

Another time, a CEO I worked with asked me to come in and build the sales strategy and the team. He had been running an 80-100 calls a day regime and claimed that this worked really well. The office environment was such that there were screens which showed by name how many dials you had made that day and how many connects etc. It was true that appointments were being made, as the sheer volume of calls meant that that would probably happen, but how many orders were being converted into business? Not many. The appointments that were made were for a demonstration that would take up to an hour, conversion was 20% or lower, and that is really not productive as a sales process.

I decided that I would switch the screens off and got each salesperson to focus on a different sector. I wasn't pushing number of calls; I was pushing quality of calls and what was in it for the client. The result was more quality conversations, more demos and conversions went up to 45% within a month. I then went away on holiday, and guess what was back in play when I returned? The screen showing everyone's call numbers. I left soon after as I knew I could not make a difference if they were so determined to continue in that way. It was a classic case of fear of change. A *we've-always-done-it-like-that-so-that's-the-way-we'll-do-it* syndrome!

I've worked for a few Sales Managers who always wanted to see call volume and rarely asked about conversion. How strange is that? Why does it matter how many calls are made if not a single person buys?

If we focus on the number of calls we make or emails we send, we're focusing on volume. We don't have time to research and tailor each call or email when we have to make 100+ calls a day. So, we make the same call to everyone and hope that someone wants to buy what we've got. We send the same email to everyone, hoping that they may just respond. Guess what? The

law of averages says you will get some sales from this method…
hopefully. But you're leaving it to chance. We leave any of our
own control or contribution to the conversation at the door. It
sees us being busy fools and working hard rather than smart.
The knock-on effect is a demotivated and exhausted sales team
– I know, I've been there! – and crabby, unhappy prospective
clients. From every angle we get the experience of sales being
hell on earth.

This myth is so damaging, and if you are setting up business, I
urge you not to fall into this trap! You might not be thinking of
opening a call centre, but you might be thinking of sending out
the same email to everyone. It's not a clever strategy and it will
make your early days in business miserable, and probably
unsuccessful. You may even find you quit. So, forget this
thinking and instead start as you mean to go on. Later on, in the
Love It part of this book, I will talk about how to lay the
foundations for quality calls and connections, so that you are
working smart not hard, and the bonus is you will love it!

Sales myth #2: Only certain people can sell

I find this one hilarious. It's so clearly untrue and it comes from
ego – from salespeople who feel they need to protect their trade
and assure everyone that it's a very difficult job and so not
everyone can actually do it.

I challenge this completely. We all possess the necessary skills to
sell. We can all sell. This is one of the central themes of this
book, so it's something we'll go into more depth later to
demonstrate. For now, suffice it to say that in some sense, we
are selling every day of our lives. From when we were very small
children we were selling. You are fully equipped to sell. Keep
reading and you will start to see that you already have strengths
and skills that are incredibly valuable when building
relationships – after all, that's what selling is.

Now, if instead of 'Only certain people can sell,' we said, 'Only certain people will want to work in sales,' that would be closer to the truth. Many people count themselves out of a sales role before they even start. But I believe that's because people have told themselves stories about what sales is and who does it. And many people running their own businesses find themselves phased by the idea of having to do the selling themselves, rather than having a team to do it for them.

But it is purely mindset that is the problem here – nothing else. I believe everyone (yes, everyone!) can love selling, if it's done in a human way. Because to be human is to sell. (More on this later!)

Sales myth #3: You need a well-defined script and a tight formula to sell

This simply isn't true, and the danger in using scripts is that you disrupt everything about human connection. People can hear that you are doing it. It feels as though you are not engaging, and you most certainly don't enter into a two-way dialogue because it is very tough to listen properly when you are reading from a script.

Scripts are often seen as a crutch. A safety net so you don't forget to mention everything about what you sell. But, in truth, sales isn't about remembering everything about everything you sell. Sales is about understanding what your client needs at that moment in time, and why. So actually, a script won't help you quite as much as you might think.

If you feel you need something to help you when you're on a call with a client, don't make it a script. Instead you could write down your top most curious questions that you want to ask them. This does a couple of things. It stops the conversation being all about you! It also prepares you to ask some great questions, which will uncover the real reasons why your client will want to buy from you. In time you will get to know your curious questions and the phrases that really help you to 'be you' when you are selling, and you won't need to refer to your list any longer.

I also see many sales methods out there which prescribe steps of the sale. Sometimes there are just a few, but sometimes there can be as many as ten or more, and it can just be overwhelming, and before you know it you are concentrating so much on what step you're on, you lose sight of what step your customer is on – possibly the doorstep about to leave!

What you need to do is take your client on a journey but not one with a set of prescribed steps. If you understand that, it becomes personal and feels much more natural. Going on a journey with your client is never forced or pushy – that sort of journey is called a kidnapping! We will talk more about the sales journey in the **Sell It** part of the book.

Sales myth #4: It's about fast talking and tricking people

This myth is probably why sales has a bad reputation. Not only is it not what sales is all about, but fast talking and tricking people are the wrong approach to take on so many levels, especially today.

The idea here is that sales is all about overwhelming people and blinding them with information and then convincing them to buy something because it will be the best for them, not even giving them chance to think or draw breath before signing up!

It is the very opposite of the approach to sales that I advocate in this book. It's about putting the client last, not at the centre, not genuinely listening to their needs, problem or challenge, let alone solving it for them. But put aside those arguments and even put aside any appeals to honesty and integrity, and the fast talking and trickery school of sales is increasingly ineffective and, if it succeeds, can be downright damaging to your brand.

People have access to so much more knowledge and information than they did in even the recent past. It is not even good strategy to just ignore this and hope that your client will not use the internet to research before making a decision.

Then let's say your fast talking succeeds. Let's say you convinced someone to buy a six-month membership to your fitness club, simply by bamboozling your lead with facts and figures so they signed up. Then they arrived at the fitness club, and it wasn't what they needed at all – they were looking for swimming sessions and your club doesn't have a pool. Even though you've got their money, they'll be unhappy. And next time your fitness club comes up in conversation they'll talk about what a waste of money it is! Fast talking and trickery rarely leaves you with happy customers. And word will spread. This is true today more than ever, given the potential influence of online reviews (including the possibility of Google reviews posted about your business) and the power, speed and reach of social media.

Sales myth #5: You have to be an extrovert to sell

Lots of people tell me they don't have the right personality to sell. They think that because they're not the life and soul of the party, or fantastic at working the room at networking events, they'll fall flat when it comes to selling. Often sales managers and recruiters reinforce this stereotype.

This belief means some people count themselves out of selling. They hold themselves back. And there are two problems with that. Firstly, sales is the lifeblood of your business. So, if you tell yourself you can't sell, you're sabotaging your work. And secondly, it means the people who need the products and services the 'non-sellers' offer, have no chance of accessing them, because you won't go out and sell them because you don't think you can!

In truth (and I know I've said this already when talking about myth #2) anyone can sell. You owe it to your business to sell.

In the next chapter I'll share some of the truths about selling, and if you're the quieter type, you'll see how your natural tendencies can become amazing sales qualities. But for now, trust me, you don't need to be a social butterfly or fond of the limelight to master human sales. You have everything you need.

Chapter 2

The Body

In this chapter we go beyond the myths to look at what we actually do, as real people, when we buy and sell. Let's start by talking about language.

Language has a huge impact on how we connect with people. If we look closely at the way language is typically used in sales, we see how scripted and unnatural it can be. When you use language that isn't your natural voice and tone, your audience will pick up on that. And it doesn't sit well with the listener to come across as being out of character and predictable.

So why is that we would want to do this? Why is it that we suddenly lose the ability to speak in our natural language when put in a sales scenario?

When we speak in life to friends, partners, our children or our work colleagues, we just chat and we are generally ourselves. There are tweaks we make. For example, we wouldn't swear or say certain words to people we don't know so well – that's just respect and politeness. But we probably don't even think about it. It's very much like driving a car. Once we've mastered driving, we don't think about our every action – we just drive. It's a subconscious action – amazing really how the brain allows us to just do it. I imagine all of you have had those journeys when you've actually forgotten making part of the trip and it's scary to wonder how you managed to get to your end destination!

Yet, when we sell we are suddenly in a mindset where we overthink. We may have fear. We may feel the underdog, have limiting beliefs, be nervous or feel out of control. Why? Because we have brought everything into our conscious mind and everything is heightened and brought to our attention.

So, my point is instead start thinking about language you use in sales as your natural language and imagine it is just another conversation – a human conversation. Add your personality to the way you say things, use words that are comfortable and be you. People buy people.

One of my clients says she thinks I sell with soul! I love this, and it says so much about how I want to help you all to sell. Sell with soul. Have a human conversation.

You will hear me say again and again that life skills are sales skills. I stand by this throughout the book and through my work and my teaching, coaching and mentoring. Sell as you. Sell with soul.

No greater place does this come into play than in language. We are all unique and whilst we may speak the same language we speak it in our own way. Now sell in that way. Now sell using that language …and not the clichéd, unnatural type of language you might think you need to use in sales.

Here are my top five phrases or words used in selling that I recommend you DON'T use. I don't believe they are phrases any of us naturally use in everyday life (but I would love anyone to contact me if they actually do – I'm always up for a challenge!)

#1: I'm sure you'll agree with me on this

Nope, I probably won't! Never assume.

#2: You can trust me!

Unless you already know the person you're talking with well, it's too soon to start talking about trust until you really have built that trust. So, don't use this early on in a conversation.

#3: I can offer you a discount

If you can offer a discount, your original price was too high! It feels desperate and devalues your product. Avoid this at all costs – there are other ways to help your customer feel like they are getting great value, which I'll cover later in the book.

#4: This offer is only available today

Most people will call your bluff on that one, and I would bet you will extend the offer if they ask tomorrow for the same deal. If you stick to it fine, but it's not the best practice and feels pushy. Also, it can damage trust if you're not careful.

#5: So, if I were to show you a way to...

As you'll see throughout this book I advocate making your conversation about your customer, not you, so use language that relates to them achieving something for themselves, not you showing them how to achieve it. For example, instead say, 'How would you feel if you were able to...'

I find language fascinating and it's such an important part of selling. Think about the language you use when selling, but think about it in terms of being natural – say things as you would naturally say them and keep it simple. We will talk more about conversations, and the questions you might ask clients, in the **Sell It** part of the book. It's one of my favourite parts of the selling journey, but for now remember the saying, 'Now you're talking my language.' It's how we connect and how we build trust.

How does the brain buy?

Let's dig a little bit deeper into what physically happens when we buy. People will often say that they make rational decisions when they buy, considering things like price, selection or convenience. But subconscious forces, involving emotion and memories, are actually at the forefront of those decisions. Technical information is processed by an area of the brain called the neocortex. This area gathers and processes information, but it has very little influence on decision-making. The decision-making area of the brain lies in a region called the limbic system, one of the oldest parts of our brain, which controls our emotions.

So, despite many of us believing that our brains make decisions through logic, our buying decisions are actually significantly driven by the emotional area of our brain. What's important for you to know is that your very first action when buying is emotional. Yes of course, the logical part of the brain can interfere eventually, but we basically create trust through our gut feel, and that is why you have to understand the buyer's 'why'. You need to tune in to the deepest need they are coming from when they are considering making a purchase.

Once you have won the emotional response over – the buyer is happy that it 'feels' like a good purchase – they will look to back their gut feeling up. This is where logic comes in. So, there is a place for talking about specifics, and features and cost, but the first decision the buyer makes is about whether they trust you.

Therefore, when it comes to selling, your fears around price, functionality or practical content do not need to be fears. What's more important is value, solution and outcome because these are much more emotional and important to the majority of your clients. If you create something of real value to your client and build a trusted relationship with them, the price is going to be a minor factor. It's not about you; it's about the client. If they see how much it's worth to them, they'll be happy to pay the price you set – and this isn't about being exploitative, but it is about knowing and owning your value!

This can be a challenge for entrepreneurs, especially if you are selling a service which you personally deliver, such as coaching or consultancy, or equally if you have personally invented or designed something tangible. We can be our own worst critics at times, with negatives thoughts like: *I'm a fraud, I'm no expert, Everyone knows what I know, No one is going to like what I've made, What if they don't need it?* and so on. So, we can add even more pressure to the sales scenario.

But, it all comes back to understanding your client and what their world looks like and we are going to fully uncover this in the **Love It** part of the book. Fear no more as you will see that not everyone knows what you know, and people do need your help. You will in fact be a complete hero to many people, because you will help them to grow their knowledge or solve a problem with the talent and expertise you have.

Statistic

70% of people make purchasing decisions to solve problems.

30% make decisions to gain something.

[Source: Impact Communications]

Think like a buyer

Before we think more about what sales is all about, let's step into the world of the buyer for a moment. What is it like to buy from you? Why would I want to buy from you? What do you give me as a solution?

I'll talk about this too in the other parts of the book, especially when I come to talk about the concept of your 'ideal client'. For now, though, let's address this from where this road trip all begins. I want to really conquer mindset. We have to be fit to travel, and if our mindset is playing any tricks on us whatsoever, we cannot move forward in the way we need to and sell in a human way.

So how do you possibly think like a buyer when you are selling? That takes a whole lot of effort. There is so much to think about and so much to worry about. And what if they don't like me? What if they think I'm not good enough? What if they think I'm too expensive? Oh my goodness, this is so stressful!

One thing I find really interesting is how we seem to forget that we are also buyers! We probably buy almost daily, if not with money, we will buy suggestions from friends, family and especially children! What happens when we buy?

There really are many reasons why people buy, and I will help you to get to the bottom of your ideal client's specific 'why' later on in the book. For now, we are looking to switch our mindset from panicking about selling and feeling fear to understanding the role of the buyer and taking control. We totally understand how buyers think – we are buyers ourselves!

Exercise

So, before I say any more, have a think yourself. Think about the last three purchases you made. What were *your* reasons for buying?

The illustration on the following pages shows some of the reasons why people will buy.

When you look at the list in the illustration, it's likely you'll spot reasons you've bought products and services in the past. It's also likely you'll see ones that are the reasons why people will buy from you.

So, all this is a reminder that we know about buying already. It's not a dark art. Keep it simple. You have a good idea why your client will buy, and you know how you buy, so start using those skills. What's interesting is that we each have a pattern we follow every time we make a purchase. Yes, it does depend on what you are buying, but the thought processes will tend to be more or less the same for you whether you're buying a tin of baked beans or a new car.

Finding out the 'why'

Exercise

Ask yourself these questions:

What is the most important thing you consider when you make a purchase?

What key thing happens for you to feel comfortable when you buy?

How do you justify a purchase?

In most cases one key word will feature in every buying decision and that word is 'value'. We like to think we will get value from something when we buy it, whether that's a beautiful meal from food we've bought, feeling fabulous from wearing those new shoes, or learning how to achieve something from the coaching we have bought. Having thought about your answers to the above two exercises, you are now firmly in the world of the buyer! That was easy, wasn't it?

A buyer's story

I have been honoured to know some senior buyers at some very large blue chip companies, and whenever we have chatted it is really clear that the battle between a buyer and a seller should never actually be a battle. It's so true that we often see the buyer as an enemy, and yet isn't it true that we both actually want to be together? Our buyer is looking for a solution and we are providing a solution – imagine the chemistry when you get this right!

Our conversations together have always concluded that buyers, even in large corporates, still have needs and want good solutions. It's not all about getting the cheapest deal. It's a whole lot more than that – they have to consider all aspects, and for that reason, they are more likely to engage with someone who actually cares about all of their needs and understands them. They see the same old mistakes over and over when salespeople come in to sell – pushing to their deadlines and their solutions, and not the buyer's.

So where does the perception of rivalry come from? It's most likely to be from trainers who have taught us over the years that it's survival of the fittest. Buyers are trained to hammer us down on price and have the upper hand! We as salespeople are taught to hold our own and make sure we get the best deal for us. Oh dear, oh dear, oh dear! Guess what? We are actually both on the same side – really, I promise. Let's apply some common sense to this. What if the buyer pushes us so hard that the deal they get is actually not good for us? It makes us no money. It takes up a huge amount of our time for no reward. It cuts corners so that we can't actually properly solve their problem or challenge. Does this make for a good relationship? A good start? Does this mean that this relationship could very likely be a long-term one? Let me help! The answer to all of these questions is NO.

The same applies if the buyer feels like we have overcharged them, didn't really understand what they needed and pushed them into something they didn't quite want. They won't feel like we understood them, and they won't see real value in what you're saying. Same questions as above – same answers, NO. And now let's take this into a life situation. Would you do this kind of deal with a friend or family member and expect to live happily ever after? The answer is NO – because in all of these scenarios we haven't understood the 'why' and stepped into the world of the buyer.

You will see as this book goes on that there are fabulous ways to connect, to step into the buyer's world and to form worthwhile relationships that are well worth taking the time to build.

It has to be said that we will never sell to everyone, but that's why when you understand this journey it won't matter to you, because you will be giving your solution to your ideal client and they will trust you to give them the outcome they need. This is good business, and the key is to walk away from business that doesn't serve you. Brave but smart.

'People buy people; people buy people they trust.'

Chapter 3

The Soul

I want to begin this chapter by, perhaps, reaching into your soul and extracting those little gremlins and voices that block us from being our true selves. They really shouldn't and don't need to. It's all about having the right mindset.

So, what might those negative voices be saying? Here are some of the things that my clients and my workshop attendees tell me about what stops them when it comes to sales:

- No one is going to want to buy what I have
- I am a fraud. I'm not an expert
- My prices are too expensive
- Everyone can do what I do
- I will come across as pushy
- I don't know how to sell
- I hate selling

And here is my flow chart which helps you to make some sense of these messages you tell yourself.

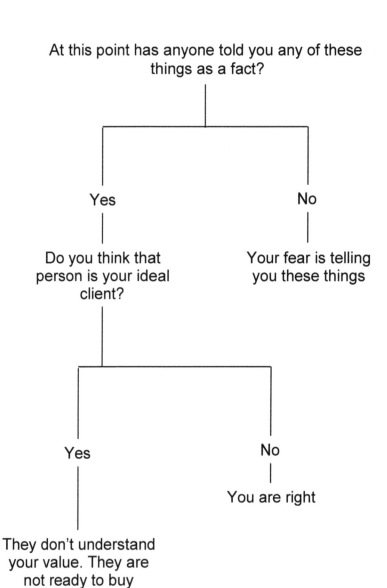

At this point has anyone told you any of these things as a fact?

Yes

No

Do you think that person is your ideal client?

Your fear is telling you these things

Yes

No

They don't understand your value. They are not ready to buy

You are right

Exercise

Write down your own list of any nagging doubts you have about selling and apply it to the flow chart.

In most cases most people won't actually get further than the first branch, which is to say that nobody has told them anything they're worried about is true, let alone someone who might be their ideal client. In other words, you are telling yourself these things and it's based on fear. Fear of change, fear of doing something different, fear of what people will think and fear of failure – and in some cases fear of success!

Here is your lesson in fear and it's a short one: You choose your own relationship with fear.

This is a powerful lesson. Learning it and changing my mindset accordingly has proved really important to me in my life.

But first let's be really clear as to what fear is all about. Understanding this is the first step to everything becoming so much clearer and easier.

Your fear is here to protect you. Its approach to keeping you safe is to like you to do what you've always done.

This explained a lot for me. Well, no wonder I never felt comfortable doing new things and no wonder I always 'future catastrophised', because fear was in control.

Another interesting fact is that the chemical reaction for excitement is the same one for fear too. So, this explained even more for me – I can choose which emotion I label this feeling as. I could choose to say I was excited, not scared.

Here's the thing – you really should be excited about sales because it is an opportunity for you to show your worth and make money. Why wouldn't you be excited and why would you fear this?

I'll tell you why, because fear has it all sewn up. You can't possibly get excited because this person may say NO. The dreaded word. You will then be rejected, which means you are no good at what you do, which means that you are a fraud, and so how can you possibly run this business? Best thing you can do is go and get a job – that's what you've always done and that's safe.

You see what I did there!

Or you can say that it was a great learning experience if someone says no, because if anything you will have learnt something. You also know you will not sell to everyone, and – who knows? – this client may come back again in the future because you read this book and did all the right things and, of course, you were the true you.

So here are my top tips for working with fear – choose the approach that works best for you:

- Reassure fear: This is what I do. 'Me and fear are in it together and it will be ok.'

- Take control of fear: Whether it's to ignore it or show it who's boss! 'I see you fear, and you can come for the ride, but I'm not going to let you take charge this time.'

- Embrace fear: Treat it like a child and look after it. 'I know you're scared and that's ok. But I won't do anything that hurts us. This will be exciting and we will still be safe.'

- Make friends with fear: Make it your ally. 'I know you're on my side, and thank you for that. I'm on my side too, so I'm not going to do anything to harm either of us.'

Whichever way you choose to change your relationship with fear, make sure you do it because then all of the things that stop you selling are dealt with.

The chart below applies this principle to the list of negative thoughts given at the start of this chapter. The right hand side column applies a different mindset.

No one is going to want to buy what I have	Your ideal client will want what you sell
I am a fraud. I'm not an expert	What is your why? (We'll go into this in **Love It**)
My prices are too expensive	Let's look at your value not price
Everyone can do what I do	Not in the way that you do it
I will come across as pushy	Understand your client's why and you won't
I don't know how to sell	Life skills are sales skills
I hate selling	You will love selling when you've read this book!

Your mindset is going to be fabulous and positive when you have completed this book because everything coming up helps you with every fear you may feel about sales. Keep reading!

There's a challenge I often set my clients, which is aimed at building a positive mindset. This is the 21 day challenge. For 21 days you commit to doing one new thing every day. It can be around gratitude, acts of kindness, trying something new, doing something for yourself, making a new connection online or offline etc. Whatever it is, you do something new every day for 21 days. It's very simple and you can keep track with a journal or even make yourself a big chart.

What's this got to do with sales, you ask? The 21 day challenge is wonderful for the mind and the soul, letting you expand what you think you're capable of. Approaching life like this will keep you grounded and allow your sales and business to flow beautifully in a human and natural way. A happy mind is a positive mind.

Life skills are sales skills

My mantra is 'Life skills are sales skills.' It seems to me that when you think of it like this it just all makes so much sense.

Let me paint you a picture of why I say what I say.

In life, we will meet new people. When we do we ask questions, we listen and we also watch all the signs of body language and eye contact, and through words we decide if someone is genuine. We don't pull out a piece of paper with a list of questions written on it and start interviewing them to see if they qualify to be our friend. This is how sales can be perceived. It doesn't have to be that way. We can sell in the exact same way as above using human conversation.

In life, when we have a problem and don't understand something we seek knowledge and a solution. To do that we will research and then we will find an expert. We will only connect with that expert if we feel they understand our challenge. We wouldn't engage with anyone who spoke to us as if they were better than us and as if we didn't know anything. This is how sales can be perceived when it is done in a pushy way.

It doesn't have to be that way. We can connect with people in a human way, show respect and use storytelling to reassure them that we know how to solve the problem when we sell.

When we really want to influence someone to do something for the right reasons we will be very honest in life. We will sell the benefits to our friends and family, and if they don't want to do something, or don't agree, we will always find out why. We ask, and we are usually comfortable to leave it if they really don't want to do something. Chances are they may still do it, or certainly will next time when they see how good it was the first time because of the stories we will tell about the experience. How many times has that happened to you?

Well, guess what? Sales is the same. Sometimes we have to be patient and we always need to know why. It's about not being rude; it's making sure we understand.

If you are a parent and your child comes to you to ask for something, you may give them an instant answer – yes or no. How many times does the child then leave quietly and exit the room? Not likely. They want to know why. And they will ask as many times as it takes until they find out the real reason. They have no fear, and as I said earlier in the book, it is only fear that often stops us being our true selves when it comes to sales.

So, remember life skills are sales skills. Think about how you behave in the situations like those described above, and now reposition that sales call as a 'virtual cuppa' and the face-to-face meeting with a potential client as meeting a new friend.

I want to end this chapter with two challenges that I sometimes set my workshop attendees. They're a good way to recap what we've covered in this chapter *and* they're great exercises to revisit at any point when you may be feeling a bit doubtful or unsure about this thing called sales.

Exercise

For the first challenge, write down (again) what scares you about sales. This time try and think what the fears are really about, even if this means stepping outside your comfort zone.

Although this may seem like focusing on the negative, the positive outcome is that finding out the core reason why you have fear around sales will help you create your own solution.

It is crucial that you are honest about what scares you about sales, because then you can address the question of how you are getting in your own way. Stepping into your stretch zone rather than staying in your comfort zone here is going to help you to grow.

Once you understand what scares you, or what you struggle with, you can start to understand how to solve this problem with the help of everything you will learn in this book.

If you are struggling with this exercise and don't quite know what might be scaring you or stopping you, then think about how you feel when someone tries to sell to you. It may be that the perception of 'sales' is getting in your way. Connect with exactly what your perception of sales is on a personal level as this alone may be the source of your fear.

Exercise

For the second challenge, think about a time when you sold yourself in life – not in your business. It may have been an interview, a charity event you organised, a competition or just meeting people within a new social group. What did you do to sell yourself? What was successful about what you did?

Why did you get the job, win the competition, make the event a success, or win acceptance into a new friendship, group or relationship?

You may have more than one example of selling yourself successfully in life, but just pick one that demonstrates your life skills well.

This exercise will help you realise that you are already a natural born salesperson.

It's important that you don't use examples of business wins – you must focus on a life win.

Why is this important? Because if you really engage with this question, you may have a 'lightbulb' moment where you realise that you have already got skills in place that you can use in sales. So, if you push yourself and dig deep, you will get the greatest benefit from this question.

What matters most is that you sell as unique you, and so your answer must be all about you and your style and your experience. That's why I'm going to buy you. Remember this: We make a client, not a sale.

Here is my example

At an interview for a new job I asked questions that I knew were related to the business I wanted to join – it showed I was interested and had done my research, and at the end of the interview I asked how I had got on and whether I would be a good fit for the company.

I got the job - why?

Because I researched the company (my potential client) asked some killer questions, and at the end I asked for feedback and ultimately asked for the job! This is sales.

Mindset is an amazing thing. Deal with fear and understand that life skills are sales skills and you will be starting to win.

I do believe you may be fit to travel the sales road trip. Let's get planning and fall in love with sales!

'When the student is ready, the teacher will appear'
                                        – Buddhist proverb

love it

Love It is really important – actually every part of the journey is important, but this part starts to be more personal. Firstly, you will get real clarity on your 'why' and your core strengths and purpose. If you are running your own business, why are you running it? What's the passion behind your drive to have your own business? It's not like running a business is an easy thing to do, so something has happened that has driven you to take this step.

I want you to feel you can trust this section of the book because much of it comes from your own instinct. You already know everything we are going to talk about here, but you may not yet have done the deeper work to start connecting it all to sales. Your key words for **Love It** are 'TRUST YOURSELF'.

There is no room in this part of the sales road trip for doubt, or even hesitation, because the true answers will come to you instinctively, so let them. This is a very rewarding and fulfilling part of the journey because it is about discovery and clarity. Imagine how when you make a journey in real life you can usually take several different routes. You may take the scenic route if it's a nice day and you feel good, and on that route you will see so many beautiful things that make it really fulfilling and enjoyable. Alternatively, you could take the fast route, which by its sheer nature is not usually very interesting and is the route most other people pick too.

The moral is take your time to get this bit right. Take your time to plan your route because you will find out so much about yourself and your business, and this will all give you the conversation to then tell people about your business and in turn do business. Brilliant!

Many entrepreneurs and business owners get their lightbulb moments in this part of the journey, which is why I call it **Love It**.

So let's begin.

Chapter 4

Love Yourself

To fall in love with sales you have to know who you are and your 'why'. Before you can understand what drives your clients, you need to fully understand what drives you.

What do I mean by your why? It's the reason you do what you do: the motivation for your business. It's what makes you unique, it's what keeps you going when things get tough, and it's why you started this whole thing.

The British-American author and motivational speaker Simon Sinek talks about your why being your 'purpose, cause and belief'. I couldn't agree more, and so the fact you may want to make money is not your why – it may be an outcome of your why, but it is not in itself your why.

Getting deep into your why is what this chapter is all about. The exercises and insights here will help you identify what you stand for, what you're proud of and what makes sure the fire in your belly is fully stoked! And once you've done that, you'll have it forever as your bedrock.

This work gives you a firm foundation for when you might start to doubt yourself. If you are ever unsure about your expertise, your abilities or whether you've got what it takes to do what you do, I urge you to revisit this chapter, to remind you to refocus on your why and the insights that will bring.

Your why, your driving force, is the starting point for marketing and selling your products and services. All of your content and offers will emerge from the clarity you'll get from digging into your why. You'll also be able to speak with confidence and authenticity about what you do, because you know exactly what you stand for.

My why is my passion for sales done in a human way – human selling. The last three years I have gone from project to project. I've worked with a number of companies, mainly SMEs, who wanted me to set up their sales strategy and build a sales team for their businesses. A perfect job for me, you might think. Yes, but only if they were going to actually allow me to put in place the strategy that I know works. Sadly, they all had the we've-always-done-it-this-way mentality, which meant that I couldn't help them that much. That made the experiences frustrating and I certainly didn't love what I was doing. Most of us work for much of our lives, so why not do work that we love – it is possible!

After losing my father in 2015, and having lost Mum in 2012, I realised that life is short and the work I was doing was not feeding my soul. Here is my why: I wanted to do work that fed my soul. It isn't about getting rich for me; it's about making a difference – showing people, who are passionate about what they are doing, how to sell in a human way. This is the most rewarding work I have ever done. This book contains all of the knowledge I am passionate about, and I can't wait for you to read it all and see what a difference it will make to your outlook, confidence and business.

So now we need to identify *your* why. This is what will get you out of bed and keep you going, it's what you talk about when people ask about your work, and it's what you'll come back to when you need to check everything's on track.

There are three approaches in this chapter to help you get crystal clear on your why. They'll get you to drill down to what's really important, what makes you stand out from the crowd and why people need to listen to you. So, grab a notebook and pen, and let your you-ness flow!

If you have done this sort of reflective and discovery work before and you think you know it, dig deep as there will be deeper reasons. The deeper you get, the more you will be different to everyone else. All of this work forms your personal brand, which is the business you present to the world. It's so important you know this, otherwise how can you sell to anyone – you won't know what you're selling!

You're about to discover exactly what is special about you and no one else in this world, because no one else is YOU! How exciting!

Let's discover your strengths

Too often we talk about the things we are not good at, the things that we *can't* do (that word again!) How often do we really focus on our core strengths? By learning about what our real true strengths are, we can adopt them, buy into them and use them to help us go out into the world. This also exercises our positive and growth mindset and gets us into the habit of talking about what we are good at – it's ok to do that!

I use this as a starting point because part of your why is made up of your strengths and what you bring to the world. I was delighted to discover a fantastic set of strength cards from a UK company called Mindspring (mindspring.uk.com). Look them up if you want to buy the actual cards – they are beautiful. These strengths are derived from the VIA (Values-In-Action) Classification from the scientific field of positive psychology. The classification resulted from a three-year dedicated effort involving 55 noted social scientists, who identified 24 character strengths that have been found to be universal – characteristics that define what's best about people.

What follows are all 24 of these strengths to help you to build the foundations of your why.

Exercise

On the following pages you will find a list of strengths and their descriptions. From these 24 listings choose your top five strengths. These should be strengths that come naturally to you and, even better, they give you energy. When you read the descriptions of these strengths they should feel like they are the 'best of you'. These we will call your 'signature strengths'.

Appreciation of Beauty and Excellence

You notice and appreciate beauty, excellence and/or skilled performance in all domains of life, from nature to art and from science to everyday experiences. If you are high in this strength, you will often experience the feelings of admiration, wonder and awe, finding richness and satisfaction in many places

If you have the strength of appreciation of beauty and excellence:

- You are likely to have been excited by excellence in music, art, drama, film, sport or science in the last month
- You admire and appreciate the strengths, talents and accomplishments of others
- You seek out new ideas and experiences that are likely to delight you
- You experience joy in other people's success

Courage - bravery

You do not shrink from threat, challenge, difficulty or pain. You have the strength to do what needs to be done, despite your fear, and take intellectual or emotional stances that might be unpopular, difficult or dangerous. Brave people also step out of their 'comfort zones' and face new experiences.

If you have the strength of courage:

* You are not afraid to speak out in the face of strong opposition
* You seek out new experiences that others might consider risky
* You'll take action to help others despite significant risk to yourself
* You often ask difficult questions that help yourself and others face reality

(NB: I like the fact that related to the root of the word 'courage' is 'encouragement', which refers literally to giving heart to another).

Creativity - originality

There are two pathways to creativity. The first involves our traditional understanding of creativity – you produce original, novel and unusual ideas and are passionate about scientific or artistic endeavours. The second path means you are outstanding at finding novel and productive ways to achieve your goals.

If you have the strength of creativity:

* You apply your imagination in new and surprising ways to solve problems
* You are rarely content with doing something the conventional way

- You enjoy producing something original
- You are open to new experiences and tend to be independent and non-conformist

Curiosity - interest in the world

Curiosity and interest in the world represent your desire for new experiences and a thirst for knowledge. You actively recognise and pursue challenging opportunities. Curious people not only tolerate ambiguity, you like it and are intrigued by it.

If you have the strength of curiosity:

- You are always asking questions, and you find all subjects and topics fascinating
- You are flexible about matters that do not fit your preconception
- You like exploration and discovery and become easily absorbed in music, movies, books, sports and people
- You are not easily bored

Fairness - equity and justice

Fairness involves giving everyone a fair chance and being committed to the idea that the same rules apply to everyone. Fair individuals treat everyone equitably, that is, in similar or identical ways and you do not let your personal feelings or prejudices bias your decisions.

If you have the strength of fairness:

- You treat everyone equally, regardless of who they might be, and believe in fair justice
- You believe that everyone deserves respect
- You have a strong sense of your own moral values and use these to guide your reasoning
- You are compassionate and tolerant towards others

Forgiveness

With this strength, you forgive those who have done you wrong or offended you. This means you are able to accept other people's shortcomings, give them another chance and resist the temptation to behave vengefully. You seek to act in a benevolent, kind or generous way to people who have done you wrong

If you have this strength:

- You don't hold a grudge for very long
- When someone hurts your feelings you manage to get over it fairly quickly
- You don't try to 'get even' when someone has upset you
- You work hard to mend relationships with people who have hurt or betrayed you in the past

Gratitude - appreciation

The strength of gratitude means you are aware of, and thankful for, the good things that happen to you in life. You do not take anything for granted and always take time to express thanks. Gratitude is both an emotion (a sense of thankfulness and appreciation) but also for good acts and good people.

If you have the strength of gratitude:

- You always say thank you, even for little things
- If you had to list everything you felt grateful for, it would be a very long list
- You are grateful to a wide variety of people and demonstrate your appreciation
- As you get older, you find yourself more able to appreciate the people, events and situations that have been part of your life history

Hope - optimism

With the strength of hope and optimism, you expect the best and have a plan to achieve it. You act in ways that are likely to make your goals a reality and remain confident that these will be achieved given appropriate effort, flexibility and positive emotions.

If you have the strength of hope:

- Despite challenges, you always remain hopeful for the future
- You look on the bright side of life and stay motivated
- You have a clear picture in your mind about what you want to happen in the future
- If you get a bad grade or evaluation, you focus on the next opportunity and plan to do better

Humility and Modesty

With the strengths of humility and modesty you are content to let your accomplishments speak for themselves and do not seek the spotlight. Humble people are honest about their limitations and the gaps in their knowledge and are content to seek advice from other people. You are able to keep your abilities and accomplishments in perspective.

If you have strengths of humility and modesty:

- You rarely talk about your accomplishments and keep a low focus on yourself
- You are open to new ideas, contradictory information and advice
- You often acknowledge your mistakes
- You have no need to present yourself to others better than you actually are

Humour - playfulness

You enjoy laughing, friendly teasing and bringing happiness to other people. With this strength, you see the light side of life in many situations, finding things to be cheerful about rather than letting adversity get you down. More than a 'joke teller' you have a playful and imaginative approach to life.

If you have the strength of humour:

- Bringing smiles to other people is important to you
- People say you are fun to be with and know they will be 'cheered up' by your company
- You try to add humour to whatever you do
- You can usually find something to laugh or joke about even in trying situations

Integrity - genuineness, loyalty

As a person of integrity, you are open and honest, living your life in a genuine and authentic way. You are comfortable with the way you present yourself and speak the truth regardless of whether it is popular or socially comfortable. It is important for you to think and act fairly with others.

If you have the strength of integrity:

- You always keep your promises and do what you say you will do. You 'walk the walk'
- You are down to earth and without pretence
- You have a strong sense of your personal values
- You tell the truth and avoid 'white' lies or omissions in information

Kindness - generosity and empathy

Kindness and generosity consist of giving your time and doing good deeds for others without expecting personal gain. Your strength of generosity means you find joy in the act of giving and helping other people, whether or not you know them well.

If you have the strength of kindness:

- You have a warm and generous attitude to other people that seems to bring them reassurance and joy
- Giving is more important than receiving to you
- You often volunteer to help others in need at work, at home and in your community, putting their needs before your own
- You get excited about other people's good fortune

Leadership

You are oriented toward influencing and helping others, directing and motivating their actions towards collective success. Individuals with this strength aspire to dominant roles in relationships and social situations yet balance this active direction with humanity for others.

If you have the strength of leadership:

- You are good at getting people to achieve things together in an efficient and friendly way
- You are often able to plan a course of action for a group, who are subsequently happy to follow you
- People look at you to help solve complex problems or resolve conflicts
- You usually take the initiative in social situations

Love and Being Loved

As a loving individual, you value close relationships with others, particularly those in which your feelings are reciprocated. You express love openly and receive it warmly, drawing strength and courage from both. You put your trust in others and make your loved ones a priority when making big decisions.

If you have the strength of love and being loved:

- There are people in your life whose happiness matters as much to you as to your own and this feeling is mutual
- You consider the people you love when you are making big decisions
- You enjoy receiving and accepting love from others
- There are people in your life with whom you feel free to be yourself

Love of Learning

With love of learning as a strength you enthusiastically seek out new information, topics and skills. You feel good when you can build on existing knowledge and/or learn something completely new. People who embrace love of learning do it for its own sake, not for an external incentive.

If you have the strength of love of learning:

- You are thrilled to learn something new
- You see opportunities to learn – anywhere and everywhere
- It is common for your expertise to be valued and sought out by others
- You do not have to be told or made to learn

Persistence - perseverance

Simply put, you finish what you start. With persistence and perseverance you have the mental strength to continue striving for goals in the face of obstacles or setbacks. This means you muster up the will to do what you say you will do – sometimes more, never less. People with the strength of persistence are dedicated, focused and patient.

If you have the strength of persistence:

- You often take on difficult projects and tackle them with minimal complaining
- You are able to see the long-term payback from your persistence
- You are not easily discouraged and work effectively towards long-term goals
- You rarely get sidetracked when you work or give into boredom or temptation

Perspective - wisdom

The strength of perspective and wisdom enables you to take stock of life in larger terms and make sense of it to yourself and to others. Perspective is the product of knowledge and experience, and the deliberate use of this to enhance well-being.

If you have the strength of perspective:

- People seek you out for advice and you listen, evaluate what they are saying and offer wise counsel
- You have a way of looking at the world that makes sense to others and yourself
- You see the big picture
- You have an accurate view of your own strengths and weaknesses, understanding the limits of what you can know or do

Prudence - sensibleness, caution

With the strength of prudence you are careful about your choices and inclined not to say or do things that might later be regretted. Prudent individuals are far-sighted and thoughtful, and you exercise caution in life. You have a flexible and moderate approach to life and strive for balance among your goals and ends.

If you have the strength of prudence:

- You think and care about your personal future, planning for it and holding long-term goals and aspirations
- You are good at persisting at activities that don't have an immediate appeal
- You have a style of thinking that is reflective and practical
- You seek a stable, balanced and unconflicted way of life

Rational Thinking - good judgement

Rational thinking is your willingness to think things through, to search actively for evidence from all sides and to weigh up evidence fairly. People with good judgement do not jump to conclusions and you are able to change your mind based on evidence.

If you have the strength of rational and critical thinking:

- You are willing to change your mind (and see it as a sign of a strong character)
- You are able to weigh your options accurately
- You seek out evidence to confirm or counterbalance your beliefs
- You rarely make snap judgements

Self-Control - self-discipline

The strength of self-control means that you can hold your responses (desires, emotions, impulses) in check when appropriate. This means you can pursue goals and live up to standards. The strength of self-discipline also means you will make yourself do something in the face of temptation.

If you have the strength of self-control:

- You rarely allow your emotions to get out of control
- You are likely to stick to your goals, such as going on a diet, giving up smoking, keeping fit etc.
- When things get difficult or complicated you don't quit or withdraw
- You are more concerned with long-term than short-term outcomes

Social Intelligence

With social intelligence you are adept at understanding the motives and feelings of yourself and other people. You 'read' people well and use this information to make people feel comfortable and valued. This means you are able to respond to other people wisely.

If you have the strength of social intelligence:

- You are able to fit in to most social situations with ease
- You are adept at influencing other people and building healthy relationships
- You are good at sensing what other people are feeling
- You are equally perceptive and honest about your own motives and feelings

Spirituality - sense of purpose

The strength of spirituality gives you strong and coherent beliefs about the higher purpose and meaning of life. You know where you fit in the larger scheme of life, and this knowledge is a source of comfort to you.

If you have the strength of spirituality:

- You can articulate your own philosophy of life, be it religious or secular
- It is important to you to have a strong purpose, or calling, in life
- You are interested in and seek out a range of values to live your life by
- You focus on behaviours, attitudes and experiences that are consistent with these values

Teamwork - loyalty and citizenship

With the strengths of teamwork and loyalty you excel as a member of a group. Loyal and dedicated, you do your share and work hard for the success of the group. At a broader level, your strength of citizenship gives you a sense of responsibility, or duty, to a common group that stretches beyond your personal interest.

If you have the strength of teamwork:

- You work at your best when you are in a group, putting the group's needs before your own
- You feel a responsibility to improve the world you live in and make it a better place for future generations
- You give up your time for the good of your town (or country etc.)
- It's important to you personally to help others who are in difficulty or in need

Vitality - zest, passion, energy

The strength of vitality enables you to approach life with enthusiasm and energy. Your zest describes your sense of 'aliveness' and you embark on tasks with a spirit of passion. Your energy is expressed not only in personal productivity and activity, but also your tendency to infectiously energise those with whom you come into contact.

If you have the strength of vitality:

- Regardless of what you do, you approach it with enthusiasm
- You never do anything halfway or half-heartedly
- You rarely feel worn out, gloomy or mope around
- For you, life is an adventure

The exercise continued

Once you have chosen your five, get feedback. Ask someone who knows you well to choose your top five strengths for you. Ask them to give you specific examples of when you use those strengths. You will find this interesting as this is how you are seen to be from the outside. Now you are building a 360 degree view of your strengths. Then settle on the final five choices. These are your signature strengths.

Next comes understanding how you use your signature strengths, when they are called upon and with whom you use them. How do they have a positive influence on your life?

Make it a task to purposefully and intentionally use one of your signature strengths each day, each week or each month. You can also use your signature strengths in different scenarios. So, as an example, if 'Curiosity' is one of your strengths and you always use it when learning, then try to use it when with new friends or in a new place. I always smile when I think about curiosity as I think it's one of my strengths, but that's because I'm just nosey! But it is how you learn, after all, and I love to empower people and encourage them to be curious.

To develop things further you can also choose to look at the strengths you don't use very often and make goals and plans to use them going forward and especially about how you could use them in your business.

You can continue to use the strengths on an ongoing basis. If you are facing a problem at work or at home, think of a strength that might help you cope with this problem. That in itself won't solve the problem, but it will act as a catalyst to understand the character strength you have and need to draw upon in dealing with the difficult situation.

And, of course, the concepts of signature strengths can be used in many other ways, for example, to enhance relationships with partners, work colleagues or family members. Get them to choose their top strengths. Give them examples of where you have seen those strengths play out. This gets everyone looking at things from this point of view.

Perhaps you can even gift people their strengths by choosing one and telling them, 'I thought of you today and this is what I think your strength is and why.' It's like an act of kindness. How about using it with your clients where it is applicable? – especially if you are a coach or providing consultation of some sort.

To sum up what we have been saying about signature strengths: identify them, challenge them, explore how others see your strengths and use them for what they are – superpowers! Make a decision to use your signature strengths consciously each and every day. They are like muscles – plenty of use strengthens their power!

Values

So now we have our strengths, we want to look at our aspirations, goals and dreams. What really feeds our soul? What work would we want to do that would not feel like work? How would you describe that work? What words would you use, what feelings would it give you and how much energy would you have from doing that work that you love?

I use the concept of 'core values' and we are just about to identify what yours are.

What's important is that you are showing up aligned with your core values. If not, then people will see through that, and in order to build the relationships that you will build in sales, people need to like and trust you. Ultimately, they will want to feel like you are an expert. If you have fear and doubts around your why, then here is where we get rid of them.

Remember we dealt with mindset and fear in **Live It**, so that is now for you to revisit whenever you need it. It's up to you to make the changes so you can feel completely at home with who you are and what you offer. Trust that this will gain you confidence and clarity in the long run.

If you are offering a service or new product, it has to be completely in line with your core values. Why? Because to sell with heart and in the most natural way, you need to truly believe in what you are selling and so it will naturally be aligned with your values. We can choose exactly how we show up in this world, so be brave enough to make the right choices for you.

Be aware that when you are selling something that isn't aligned with your core values you show up in a very different way. It will be reflected in your energy, your language and even the care with which you sell it. You will hear me quote this regularly because I want you to understand how important it is. **People buy people, and people buy people they trust**. It's a tough call to build trust when you yourself don't believe in what you're selling.

I can honestly say that I have put together programmes and concepts that I didn't end up selling because they didn't feel right. For me that's very much value-based, and you know what feels right and true.

Identifying your values

Your values are part of what makes you unique. They are what make you the 'true you'. What's most interesting is that we all know what our values are because they have been built since we were tiny. Our parents may have taught us things, teachers may have taught us things, but in any case the way we see the world is built from experience and from when we were very young. If asked about your values, you may find it hard to list even just five of them because they are also often disrupted by what we think our values should be based on media, society and opinion. That's why we have to trust what our personal values are.

Exercise

Rather than feed you a list of words that you can then select from, I want you to take yourself to a quiet place, so you can really clear your mind to do this exercise, and I want YOU to come up with your five core values.

You'll find some notes to help you with this below.

Here's something to help you.

Think of a time when you had great success. A time when you really excelled yourself and were very proud of what you had achieved.

What were you feeling?

What was going on?

What values were you honouring then?

Like anything you also have to look at the opposite side of this too – it really helps. So, think to a time when you were frustrated, angry and, in your eyes, perhaps you failed.

What were you feeling?

What was going on?

What true values did you abandon?

Now think about what you need in your life, besides basics like food and drink.

What must you have in your life to experience fulfilment?

What helps you to create self-expression?

What gives you a strong level of health and vitality?

What makes you feel excitement and adventure?

What values are so important to you that you would feel incomplete without them?

Now you will see that you have made your own list of values! All by yourself, and those are your true values, not someone else's list.

> ## The exercise continued
>
> The next step is to put them into categories as this will give some breadth to where they have come from. *So, what are they all related to?*
>
> Again, you'll find some material below to help you.

For example and to help you categorise your list:

Values like accountability, responsibility and timeliness are all related to each other – they are **practical-based values**.

Values like learning, growth and development also relate to each other – they are **aspirational values**.

Values like connection, belonging and intimacy are also related – they are **emotional values.**

Now that your list is categorised, you can use it to help see what is really important to you.

> ## The exercise continued
>
> Choose five to ten values from the list that are the most important ones to you. These we'll call your core values. The number of them can vary from person to person. But if you choose less than five, then you risk not acknowledging the depth you have; and if you pick more than ten, the list will risk lacking focus.
>
> Once again, you'll find some help with this below.

To help compile your list of core values, ask these final questions:

What values are essential to your life?

What values represent the true everyday you?

What values are essential to supporting your integrity?

To cement these values, for each value you can make a statement for yourself to help you to confirm why you picked that core value. So, one of my core values is 'Contentment' and my value statement could be, 'Contentment: to live every day knowing I chose how I want to feel.'

And why is this important work?

Your core values are the ones that will help you on your **Live It, Love It, Sell It** journey. Your core values are the reason you are doing what you do, so trust them and carry on. Avoid fear telling you that you should be doing something else. Take the chance. Remember if you totally believe in your values and the solution you provide, then your client most certainly will too.

Your story is a vital connection to your business

Storytelling is a crucial tool in establishing your brand, and in sales people connect with stories because we are naturally curious about each other. We have heard stories from a very young age and we relate to them. We love the anticipation of what happens next. When people see power and passion in an authentic way they want to listen, are more engaged, and connect with you and your message. Getting clear on your story will also get you clear on your mission and your why. From this comes your content and the messages you go out into the world with.

A great storyteller will make a connection and show they are truly engaged with what they believe in. They will have a backstory to share. They will be real and relatable and they will be open about their mistakes along the way.

You have a story and it is the reason why you have started your business. If you run your own business, there is usually a defining moment when you made that decision that you would be the owner of your own business. We can all do anything if we want to, but often something will trigger the action we take. It could be that you lost your job through redundancy and so had some available funds. You could have got to a point where you no longer thought you could work in such a restrictive environment, or maybe you just wanted to do something completely different and work with a life passion you had never been able to enjoy in your working life.

Your story is the key ingredient of your business why.

My story could start in a few places. Sales was part of my life from the age of 16 when I started my first job at Nat West Bank. Alongside that, I had a bar job for extra money and I was an Ann Summers manager with a team of consultants as well as selling at parties of my own! This was all quite a lucrative time in my life, and looking back it could, of course, be considered the start of my entrepreneurial journey.

However, I think of my story beginning when I had my son, Sam, on New Year's Day 2005. He was actually due on Boxing Day, but he decided to keep me hanging on for a few more days. So, my New Year present was this beautiful little boy and I had never felt love like it before.

This changed my whole outlook on life. At the time I had been working in my husband's (now ex-husband) business selling incentive schemes to corporates. I promptly announced that I didn't want to do that anymore and what I really wanted was to be with Sam! On a serious note, though, I knew I needed to still work as I was driven and couldn't imagine not working; I needed a purpose for me as well as the purpose of being Sam's mummy, so my Truly Madly Baby story began right there. This was the business I took into *Dragons' Den*.

People often want to hear about this, and at conferences or events I sometimes talk about Truly Madly Baby. I talk about why it started, how my own baby was the catalyst and the adventure I had, from appearing on *Dragons' Den* and winning investment from Peter Jones to continuing to build Truly Madly Baby into a £1 million business with global enquiries, and then finally losing everything – absolutely everything – when I didn't really need to.

When I think about the key factors in my story I can talk about entrepreneurship, hard work, multi-tasking in life, building a business, networking, PR, winning awards, going out of my comfort zone, getting back up having fallen down – down to the very bottom of my hell, going back out into the world and being interviewed for jobs, and building a career again from nothing at the age of 40 as a single mum. I can talk about grief, resilience and determination. Always seeing the positive in what I did and knowing that today I am built from every mistake I made. I couldn't do what I do today if it hadn't been for my story. I couldn't have written this book if it hadn't been for my story.

This might seem like a rocky road, but to me it's not a doom and gloom story. It's a source of enormous strength and learning and I wouldn't be me without it.

When you are thinking about your own story, it might help to consider the following questions to bring out the important stages:

1.   What was the starting point of your story?

2.   What was the inspiring moment or 'need for change' moment?

3.   What happened at the turning point for change to occur?

4.   What is your amazing solution you offer the world as a result of your story?

Your story is your sadness and your joy, but for the audience it has to be about what's in it for them too. What have you found out that you can then give back to them? How can you inspire them? Throughout this whole book I will always tell you that it will always be about the client and not about you, but critically it is your story that makes what you have to offer authentic and powerful. It is something for your client to connect with, and probably recognise something of themselves in.

Everyone has a story and I will share more stories with you as we go through this book together. Out of adversity comes some amazing businesses, some amazing women and men.

I spoke at the Entrepreneurial Leaders Live conference in Summer 2018, curated by the inspiring business coach Helen Packham. One of the key themes of the event was how critical your story is to your business. Without a story, you're not you. And without you, there's no business.

Clarifying your own story is a great thing to do because it will make it clearer to yourself why you are the expert when it comes to what you offer.

Exercise

Think about your story in your mind. Start at as many different points as you want because each time you do you discover something more about your why. Then write your story down or record it. Refer back to it and become so familiar with it that telling it becomes as natural as breathing.

How you can use your story

Once you've shaped your story, it can be used to connect with your audience in so many ways. For example, through:

- your website copy (particularly on your 'About' page)
- introducing yourself on social media
- a Facebook Live or Instagram Story
- a blog
- a speech or talk
- an interview
- a podcast
- your regular content out to the world

You might not feel like the hero of your story, and the thought of talking about it might feel uncomfortable. So remember this – your story isn't for you; it's for your clients! By sharing your story with your ideal client, you are helping them see the potential for their own story – *they* are the heroes! This whole process repeats again when it comes to your clients. Find out their story as this is where you will connect, your stories will resonate with each other and you will form the relationships that lead to sales.

Remember you tell as many details as you want about your story. I say this because some of my clients have said to me that they don't want to tell things warts and all – so don't. It's about connecting to someone so you know how they feel. You've been where they are once before. Whether you offer a product or a service, you can show that you understand because you've had a similar experience. That is all done through your story.

Storytelling will work for you throughout the whole of the sales road trip. It will give you confidence as you work through your life skills and mindset (**Live It**) as it will help you realise what a great story you have.

Here in **Love It**, it will help you to develop your core messages and content and the reason you are doing what you do, and how that connects to your ideal client's pain or challenge. It will also serve you well when you begin to sell (which we'll come onto in **Sell It**).

Storytelling in sales runs through the whole journey. It's a foundation to keep returning to if you find yourself in doubt about anything.

When you are thinking about your why here are three examples of ways that you can use storytelling to its full advantage.

First, it can be used to illustrate where you were at a point in the past and to contrast that with where you are now. This can be great for encouraging others to do the same and works brilliantly in emails and posts on social media.

Here's an example from my own life:

After Truly Madly Baby got taken away from me I felt totally lost and defeated. I'd worked for years to create a global, thriving business that I totally believed in. I loved the women I worked with, I loved the products, and I knew the business model was spot on for where I wanted to go. But I lost it all due to trusting the wrong person. I felt exhausted, I felt cheated and it all felt so unfair. I even felt sorry for myself; I'm not going to lie.

But, even in that terribly dark place, I knew I had a choice. I could give up which would mean looking for any job just to earn some money, which would give me no personal satisfaction – this option was safe and would allow me to keep my head down and lick my wounds. Or I could pick myself up and get back out there – do what I knew I was good at, connecting people with the products, services and goods that helped them. Something otherwise known as selling! So, that is exactly what I did. I got back into sales and got the ten years of experience I needed to do what I do now.

I started back on the road again, doing what I had done ten years before then, and so again I proved myself and ended up leading a team of my own. Not only that, the team when I inherited them were on their knees, £2 million off target with no hope of gaining ground. Within 18 months we had smashed our target, pulled back the revenue we needed and were celebrating bonuses and a big hit. How did I do it? Through focusing on the human side of selling – the why, the strengths of the individuals and the absolute human team spirit.

Now I'm doing what I truly love – helping people on a mission with the confidence and skills to get out there and sell! None of that would have happened if I'd stayed small, played the victim and decided that the universe had it in for me.

Second, your telling of your story can be used to illustrate the moment you finally come up with the solution to a problem. It may have been a moment of clarity in the bath, but what you came up with is really going to help them. Often these 'eureka' moments come when you strip everything back to basics and build from there. It's a great way to launch a new product or service.

Here's my example:

My job after losing my business was at a venue. I had been selling on the road again, but in a short space of time I was promoted into a Head of Sales role, which was great, but, as just explained, I found myself heading up a team that was missing targets. To make matters worse, we were in the middle of a recession. Making a difference was going to be no mean feat!

I had to think about how I was really going to make a difference and start to inspire and energise the team. My eureka moment was when I realised it's actually all about keeping it simple. I got to know every one of the team of 14 very talented salespeople on a one-to-one level and found out what their strengths were. I then nurtured those skills with coaching and mentoring so that everyone knew the part they played in the team – their why and the business why. This was the first time they had really worked as a team and it had fantastic results. I also split our selling areas into territories by postcode. This meant they had focus. With targeted areas and knowledge of their why and the business why, they started to sell the venue in a human way. That's just what this book is all about – that same journey.

A third example of a way in which you can use telling your story to its full advantage is by using metaphors. This is a great way to relate a concept you're comfortable and familiar with to an audience who don't understand it so well. It's a good way of teaching and clarifying.

Here's my example:

I use the term 'sales road trip' as a metaphor. **Live It, Love It, Sell It** is that sales road trip broken down into parts of the journey. The beginning, the middle and the end. Simple, right? –

Yes. The **Live It** part of the journey is the beginning where we make sure that you are fit to travel. The middle of the journey, **Love It**, is where you plan out the route for your journey so that you arrive at the right destination. Then **Sell It**, well that is actually how you travel that journey without getting lost or breaking down!

Your personality

Tapping into the core elements of your personality is a fantastic way to show up as your true authentic self. As we know, people buy people, and so if you are being anyone other than yourself, your audience picks up on that. Even if they don't pick up on it, they may not be able to see the sides of you that they need to in order to be inspired by you and take action and ultimately work with you.

It isn't easy showing up fully. It takes time, and you can feel exposed and worry what people might think. One of the biggest things we do is presume that people are judging us. The good news is, as we talked about in **Live It**, we now know that our fear plays a huge part in this and, more importantly, what to do about it!

Let's talk about the important parts of your personality to use when it comes to business and, indeed, sales.

Exercise

Take a moment to write down the answers to these questions. As always, asking your friends or colleagues can also be very helpful.

- What are you like when I first meet you?

- What are you like when you are at your best?

- How are you with people you really like and connect with?

- What is it about other people that resonates with you?

- What were you like when you were a child?

- How are you when you feel completely free?

- What would you do if you had no fear?

Once you have answered those questions, you will have a good picture of your personality. You are unique. There is only one you, and you will be one of the key reasons why people buy from you.

Why authenticity matters

The definition of 'authentic' is genuine, real, not false, not copied. When we try and be something we are not people can tell and more importantly so can we. The signs will scream from us: body language, eye contact, language, how we behave and how we react. All of these elements are key factors of selling and building rapport. This is why I believe life skills are sales skills. If we are not authentic, we won't connect with our clients.

A buyer relies heavily on trust. If they like you and feel you are authentic, genuine and real, then there is a good chance that they will trust you. When they trust you there is a good chance they will buy.

The secret to all of this is understanding your why. Now you have done the exercises – You have, haven't you? Go back and do them if not! – and have your strengths, values, story and personality at your fingertips, you will naturally be able to talk about it with confidence and in an authentic way.

The exercises in the next chapter will then help you understand your ideal client and their why. When you start to match the two you can stop second guessing. You can stop doubting and you can begin to be the real genuine you. Your client will see that, and they will understand that you know what you are good at, you understand their problem or challenge and you can actually solve it! Belief, rapport, trust. A human conversation. Powerful stuff.

When you are selling one of the golden rules is: It is not about you; it's about your client – always. But they have to trust you, and the way to do that isn't through trickery or clever techniques. It's by being genuine, honest and trusting yourself. Do this work and you will no longer fear selling.

We have seen how common sales fears are centred around things like the following:

• No one is going to want to buy what I have

• I am a fraud. I'm not an expert

• My prices are too expensive

• Everyone can do what I do

• I will come across as pushy

• I don't know how to sell

• I hate selling

When you did your work on your mindset, strengths, values and personality and looked at your why this answered all of those doubts. This now allows you to be you and tell your story, which is yours and no one else's. Now you can see that being you is great. Being you is authentic and real.

Let me just reassure you again with answers to the doubts above

- Your ideal client will want what you sell

- What is your why?

- Let's look at your value not price

- Not in the way that you do it

- Understand your client's why

- Life skills are sales skills

- You will love selling when you've worked through this book!

Whatever happens you are human, as we all are, and so the greatest gift you have is the art of human conversation. Step into your client's world and build rapport. Empathise, recognise and realise that you can relate to their problem. Everyone wants to talk about themselves, but there is something special when someone wants to talk about you with you.

So, look at how far you have come now that we are at the end of this chapter.

- You know your signature strengths

- You know your core values

- You have identified your story and where it links to your business and your clients

- You have learnt how to use that story without it feeling yucky and too revealing and personal.

Now start thinking about all of this on a daily basis. Use affirmations, statements about you and your life **said in the present tense**.

- I am great at what I do

- I can sell

- I have an amazing business

- People love what I do

Why do these work so effectively? Because they reprogram your brain and give you a positive focus.

Make it a habit to understand your why, so you know it inside out and it flows naturally. Now you are doing business as the true you with confidence, and it will feed your soul!

Chapter 5

Love Your Clients

Now that you've tuned in to what drives you in business, and what you can be proud of about yourself, we need to focus on the other important person in this conversation: your client!

In business it's as important to rule people out as much as attract the ones we want to work with. Your message and the solution you offer will be so much more powerful if you've identified who you're here to help and make sure you aim your pitch at them.

A powerful way to do this is by creating avatars, or fictional people, representing your ideal clients. Now, if you've been in a corporate environment, or you've been in business for a while, you may well have generated avatars before. They are also sometimes called personas. You may even be rolling your eyes and thinking, 'Done this before, tell me something I don't know!'

But here's the thing. If you've read through the earlier chapters of this book and done the exercises, it's likely you've made some shifts, or at least reminded yourself of why you're in business in the first place. You'll have awakened some powerful life skills – life skills are sales skills, remember – and you'll know that you're selling something you have a genuine interest in and are proud of.

I say all of this because it's possible that you or your ideal client has changed. So, even if you think you already know who your ideal client is, I'd encourage you to take another look at this now. I also want to give you some new ideas on this that I believe are even more important than just knowing WHO your ideal client is. Read on and it will make sense.

If you're doing this for the first time, that's great too. This is your chance to really bring to life the person you want to work with.

Exercise

So, first of all let's have a think about these questions:

- If you could help anybody with your product, service or idea, who would it be?

- When people hear what you do, what do they ask you?

- What are the top questions you get asked all the time by your clients?

- What field are your current clients in?

- What solution do your clients provide?

- What are the goals of the clients you currently have?

- What specific results have your top clients achieved already (if applicable)?

- Do your clients really know what they need or have they only identified what they want?

The last question in the exercise is interesting as we often think we need something and actually we are not focusing on the right thing. I have come across this with my own one-to-one coaching clients. Sometimes someone will tell me that they just want help with selling their solutions. That's great and I will take that on board because it is all about the client, but I will explain that the **Live It** work is so important as a place to check in and make sure you are fit to travel. If there were a mindset issue that I left uncovered, then it could sabotage the **Sell It** work. So, **Live It** is always a check in place and that's how I position it. This just adds value, and shows I care.

Exercise

Think about what the solution you provide looks like right now. What do you help people with? And what have your clients tried in the past that has NOT worked for them?

Write down ideas for three different areas where you could help your ideal client to achieve specific outcomes.

For example, my answers might be:

1. I help people get clarity on their why

2. I help people to understand the sales skills they already possess

3. I help people to sell in a human way to gain confidence and fulfilment

---

So, now we've started thinking about your ideal client and what you can do for them. It's time to dig deeper to see how we can really connect with this ideal client.

Describing your ideal client

Describing your ideal client helps you to look at even more specifics and something really interesting happens when you do this – I'll ask you about this at the end of this stage!

Now you have to dig deep because I really want you to step into their world. If we don't do this, we will never really understand where they are right now. What is their real challenge and pain?

Exercise

Think about who would make the most perfect of clients to work with. This may be someone you have worked with before, or it could be someone you would love to work with.

Now clear your mind and step into their world and imagine you are them. Think about when Alice entered the world through the looking glass. Imagine, like Alice, you have stepped into another world, but for you it's the world of that client and you are them. This world will feel different, but try and experience it as though you were truly stepping into your client's shoes.

How does it feel to be in that world across a 24-hour period? What emotions do they experience and what challenges do they face? What do they need and what are they lacking? What would make that world amazing and a real joy to live in?

When you answer the next set of questions answer them as if you are them. Imagine and feel every answer. I recommend you take care to really find a quiet time to do this when you will be undisturbed. It's a very valuable exercise that will give you lifelong value once you've done it.

So here we go – you are now your perfect client.

All the questions below are written in the form of asking about you, but that 'you' is not you but your ideal client. The exercise is to answer the questions standing in their world for the reasons described above.

How old are you?

Are you single or married?

Do you have children? How many? How old?

What do you do for work?

What is your job role?

How much do you earn?

Where do you live? Is it a city, town or village?

What type of home do you live in?

Do you rent or own your home?

What do you do in your spare time?

What holidays do you enjoy? In what locations?

What products and services do you like?

What would you HAPPILY pay for?

What will you NOT buy for the sake of it?

What factors influence you to buy?

What puts you OFF buying?

Describe your personality in three words?

Now, to help you dig even deeper, the next set of questions focus more on the emotional side of your ideal client:

What delights you?

What makes you cross?

What are you really good at?

What are you not so good at?

What stops you moving forward?

What is the cost to you for NOT doing those things?

What do you regularly worry about?

What causes you the most stress right now?

How are the relationships with your loved ones?

How do you feel about yourself as a whole, physically, emotionally?

How do you feel about your self-worth?

What three things would be on your wish list right now?

What would your best friend tell you about yourself?

What does your world look like in 12-months' time?

You'll have noticed how the questions in the exercise don't just cover the buying habits of your ideal client and their areas of need, but cover all sorts of lifestyle factors too. This is important – it helps you put yourself in their shoes, see them as a whole person and, ultimately, connect with them better, which gives you a huge advantage in getting that sale. The exercise is important and relevant no matter what you sell. Remember that corporate ideal clients are still human, so all of this is applicable to them too. To know your client on an emotional level is very powerful and builds trust and connection.

So, let me ask another question about your ideal client now:

Is it someone just like you?

Most people say, 'Yes, it is.' How amazing is that? You are often, in fact, your ideal client, or you certainly were once. That's why you are winning already because often your ideal client was you before you started your business, you before you realised and learnt everything you now know in order to be able to offer the solutions you can now provide. This is why you are the perfect expert for them to work with, whether your solution is a product or a service. The solution was born from that time when you were once your perfect client. Magic right there and a lightbulb moment for many!

Market research

Market research helps us get to know our ideal clients in an even deeper way. A powerful approach is to pick your favourite five clients of the last year and ask them whether you can pick their brains via Skype or over a coffee. Or if you don't have clients yet, ask people who you'd like to be your clients in the future. Often people are happy to give their time for free – it's amazing how much people are happy to talk about themselves and how they'd like to improve their lives!

A similar approach works for gathering larger datasets via survey too. Think about where your ideal clients hang out online: Facebook or LinkedIn groups, Twitter, your own email list. Then create a quick survey to find out more about what makes them tick, what they love about what you do and what keeps them up at night.

Your survey questions will depend on your business, but a key rule to ask great questions is to always think about your solution when you think about what question you want to ask. For example, my solution is that I help you to fall in love with sales. So, a question I can ask is what is the first thing you think when someone says the word 'sales'? This is a great question because it brings out all sorts of emotions and blocks and needs and challenges, and straight away I know I can help because my solution addresses all of these.

You get the gist.

Obviously, focus on the people you really want to serve here! Don't survey everyone just to get loads of data. Focused data has more value. It adds to your knowledge of your clients, old and new, and helps you understand their world.

Niche

I want to address this word while we are talking about the ideal client. 'Niche' has become something of a buzzword, as such words do, which means it will fall in and out of fashion and likely feel altogether a bit yucky to some people.

I recently read that niche is all about defining the four areas that you 'niche in':

- **physical area** – the area you operate in or sell to (local, national, specific countries etc.)

- **audience** – the audience or customers you're targeting (specific ages, interests etc.)

- **price point** – the price point of your goods (designer, affordable, budget-friendly etc.)

- **delivery method** – the way you go about selling or offering your products/services (via subscription, with a membership option etc.)

This is all fine and could help you to really focus on who your business serves, but I think it's easier to tell you my recommended considerations when you 'niche'. I like to keep it simple.

It's not about choosing a niche – it's about clarity of your why, who you want to help and the value you provide with your solution.

If you truly nail this, you have a niche right there. It's true. So, let's forget the buzzwords and let's get to the real heart of selling, and **Love It** tells you everything you need to know about your niche.

Chapter 6

Love Your Value

Now you're clear about what you love about you and your business (Chapter 4) and what you love about your clients (Chapter 5) it's time to connect the two.

Identify your client's WHY

This is where we journey even deeper into your client's world. Really getting to grips with what they care about, why they're here and what problems they have.

You will hear me talk about this in various parts of the book as it's critical to getting a natural sale. For example, when we talk about building rapport I don't focus on some of the typical subjects you may have experienced in traditional sales training like body language, eye contact and tone of voice. Yes, those things are a part of it, but they will naturally happen in your subconscious and by bringing focus onto them things can become quite unnatural. Rather than worry about how you should be looking, moving and talking, the most effective sales technique I know is to relax and be you.

This is now all about your client, so I want you to really imagine what it is like to be them. You have to see everything from their perspective, even if you don't agree with it or can't necessarily understand it. But don't get too worried about this. Often entrepreneurs will work with clients or customers they have something in common with. (And many of us have already identified that our ideal client is a former version of ourselves, so it's just a case of remembering how you felt when you were at that point.)

Being able to step into your client's world is one of your strongest assets when selling. It creates trust and empathy. Imagine if you had a problem and someone was totally in your world, listening and imagining how it feels, looks, what effect it has, how frustrating it can be, how stressful it is, how it affects you, and so on. How much more likely would you be to follow their advice, and more importantly trust them?

It feels great when you know someone truly gets you. Think about this in life as well as business. Think of people who have this wonderful gift of just making you feel like they really care and understand why you feel how you do. That's the sort of person you're going to be.

I've said it before, but I hope you are doing the exercises in this book and not just reading through. Unless you give this your all and find time and space to allow yourself to get out of your zone and into theirs – just like you did when you worked on your ideal clients – you will never be able to sell your solution in the most authentic way.

Heaven and Hell

You now know your why, your core values and your ideal client – what they really look like in detail. These are your foundations for business and for selling with ease. Now we are moving to the next stage, which is where the magic really starts to come together – with your client's journey.

To fully help your ideal client, you need to move them from a place of pain to a place of pleasure. This I call Hell to Heaven. I could put it like this: You have to acknowledge the hell in order to sell!

We now want to plot the journey of your ideal client, and we start with what their hell looks like. From a sales perspective, your client is starting off in some sort of 'hell'. There is some challenge, pain or friction in their lives, big or small, which they want a solution for.

Tuning into this bad feeling, this point of unease, is key to helping your client to the greatest degree. When you can step into their world and witness how they feel, you'll get a full, sensory understanding of what it is they need and how you can help them.

What is their ultimate challenge or pain and how does it make them feel? You need to step into their world and really feel what this is like. Only this way can you begin to see how you can help them, which is ultimately why they will come to you.

We then want to explore exactly what it will look like when they have the solutions to their challenges and pain. How will it feel and how will it change how they do things and help them to move forward? How will their life be different? What is the outcome for them if someone waved a magic wand?

When you have a picture of both ends of the scale you can map a complete journey that you can then take your ideal client on, to move your client away from their pain and towards their outcome. From here you can start to define your products and services – but hold that thought for now.

First let's go from Hell to Heaven.

Exercise – Hell to Heaven

For this exercise we want to bring things to life. It works best with a large area to work on, a double page spread of a notebook, or a whiteboard or a large piece of plain paper in landscape aspect - and to make it more visual you can even use coloured pens. I have some magic whiteboard paper, which is amazing. You can stick it on any wall and then write on it – great for exercises like this!

On your piece of paper, or whatever you're using, draw on the left hand side the word 'HELL' and on the right hand side 'HEAVEN'. Make it big as this allows you to really open your mind as to how your ideal client feels, to what their world looks like.

Hell

You are now in your ideal client's world. Visualise and feel it. What are the biggest problems they are currently experiencing? This is their hell. Here they will feel lost, stuck, frustrated, emotional. Remember we have covered elements of this in the previous ideal client exercise, so use the work you have already done. Under the word 'HELL' write down all the emotions that they may be feeling and experiencing. I really want to focus on emotions as this is how we connect as humans. Even better, if you have once been them, write everything down you remember feeling, seeing, doing and wanting.

As an example, one of my ideal client's problems is that they just don't know where to start with sales and yet the lifeblood of their business is sales – without sales they make no money. This is stressful, so stressful as to make them feel paralysed, lost and not able to take any action. It stops everything, and I mean everything. This feeling of being lost means they actually start to doubt what they do, they don't know who they are selling to, and they don't even know how they can help anyone. The knock-on effect is they start to future catastrophise too, thinking things like, *If I can't sell anything, I won't be able to afford my mortgage and then I will lose my house and then I may have to get a job and what if I can't get a job - what will I do then?*

Do you recognise this? It's an example of their mindset being in the wrong place. It's someone in need of the work we did in **Live It** and the rest of the work we've done so far. When you go through this work everything, instead, makes sense. You simplify that whole process of what you are selling and to whom and you feel happier, more confident and you become human.

Get as much detail down as possible about their 'hellish' feelings. This will be absolute magic for unlocking how you can help them! And, again, this will give you brilliant content for blogs and posts on your social media as well as discussion pieces and storytelling.

Heaven

Now move over to 'Heaven' and imagine how your client will feel once you have helped them and provided them with a solution. What will have changed? What will the knock-on effect be for them emotionally, practically? What will their big picture now look like? What possibilities are now available to them? What difference will it really make to their business, life or journey? Take time to put as much as you can down – explore every avenue. Plot this in any way you wish. You may want to draw pictures, write words, use phrases… this is your exercise. There is no right or wrong with this – what is important is that you step into their world and use your imagination in the greatest way you can.

For example, in my business I imagine my ideal client calling me to say that they have done everything I had told them about and telling me how interesting it had been to define all of these areas. It had made them really realise their core values and had helped them see very clearly who their ideal client was and actually why they could help them. Through doing this, they reached their sales target for the first month, and they had realised that selling was just a human conversation! An ultimate lightbulb moment – amazing! I actually have testimonials that talk about these points. It's so rewarding.

The other huge thing that the Heaven and Hell exercise achieves is the amount of content it gives you. You will see when we come to **Sell It** that all of this exercise creates subject matter for how you go out into the world. Hold that thought, but keep all of this work safe so you can always go back to it. There is so much value here.

The value journey

We now use all of the work you have done to create your value journey.

THIS IS YOUR SERVICE and the PRODUCTS you will offer! So where do you come in? As a business owner who loves what they do, your job is to provide a solution for your client, taking them from their hell to their heaven. And you do it all through what you offer: your products and services.

This is how you are going to get them to where they want to be. What you will offer will help to enable the changes they need to make or solve the challenge they have. You will come to see your products and services not as things you are trying to push onto people but as valuable tools that can move them away from a place of discomfort, stress and worry to a place of ease, happiness and freedom. And this way it's so much easier to sell them wholeheartedly!

You'll start to see the real value in what you are providing. It's very easy for us to sit and wonder if all of this 'stuff' we know is of value or use to anyone. We might do that because it's easy for us to understand and we already know it. But, just like you are reading this book because you want to know about selling and might be stuck or afraid, your own clients will feel a similar need about the expertise and products and services you provide.

So, if you asked me to design a logo, I would probably go into meltdown, draw a blank and more to the point I would have no idea of where to start. I'm not a graphic designer. Now a designer or marketer will look at it and it will be a piece of cake. No doubt they might use some sales techniques like stepping into my world! But they will not find it difficult and it will hopefully feed their soul to create an identity for my business. What's even more important is this: I as their client will have to completely trust them, and trust that they understand my business and my ethos and values, because I don't have the skills to do it myself, or maybe I just don't have the time. There is that word 'values' again!

So, now you can take all the points from the Heaven and Hell exercise and block them into three key areas that encompass everything you can help your client with. I suggest three because in so many places we see three appear. It sits well with us psychologically. So, a story has a beginning, a middle and an end. There were three kings in the Christmas story, three bears with Goldilocks and three musketeers etc. As children we learnt

A B C and 1 2 3. So, it is quite clear that our brains are comfortable with and used to threes.

In fact, my entire business is built around three concepts, the three key concepts in this book: **Live It, Love It, Sell It**. For each of these, there are significant issues I can help clients with to move them from their hell to their heaven.

At this point, let's just do a sense check on this to make sure we are all following the thread of it.

Live It is about making mindset shifts and developing a personal skills mindset, eliminating fear and getting you fit to travel the sales road trip.

Love It is about understanding your why, the ideal client and their why. This is in order to plan that journey and keep a focus that won't make sales seem like an overwhelming thing. It's about you connecting with your ideal client because your solution matches their need.

Sell It – the third and final part that we will come to shortly – is the practical sales journey, which is critical in order for you to get to your destination. It's about being visible, storytelling and showing your value.

If you miss any steps, you may find that your client will take a wrong turning! Not good and you lose control of the journey – and remember you are the driver.

The 'hell' feelings of my ideal client might fall against the need for **Live It, Love It, Sell It** as follows.

Live It: lack of confidence, uncomfortableness, doubt, imposter syndrome, limiting beliefs, feeling overwhelmed, not feeling good enough, negative past experiences etc.

Love It: not knowing who their ideal client is, not knowing what they are selling, not knowing why anyone will want to buy what they offer, not knowing what their value is, doubting they actually have anything to offer etc.

Sell It: not knowing how to sell, not knowing where to start, worrying about what to do if nobody buys, worrying about negotiation or objections etc.

Now think of the ways that you can help your client overcome their 'hell' feelings with the service you have to offer. What do you offer and what knowledge do you have that will guide them and support them from their hell to their heaven? It's amazing how you will start to see what you know and the expertise you naturally bring as a solution for your clients. How much does this boost your confidence and continually improve your mindset around sales? Don't be frightened to break this right down into small pieces of advice and one-off subjects, especially if you're a trainer or coach, or even individual products and components. By getting into the fine detail you can also start to see how things you offer naturally go together, and that's how you build product ranges, programmes, course subjects and service levels and, of course, how you add value.

In my case I am able to design varieties of my product to address all of my clients' hell issues. These can take the form of:

- one-to-one intensive coaching and mentoring

- group programmes with the sales starting basics

- membership of a group with regular short-burst training

- online courses

- workshops

- inspirational public speaking – talking about sales, business and, of course, the fact that there's no such word as can't

- this book!

- and podcasts - I have a podcast called the 'The Human Conversation' on iTunes – check it out!

(You can find out more about all these by visiting my website: liveitloveitsellit.co.uk)

All of these products and services address the issues I came up with in the Heaven and Hell exercise when applied to my ideal client. Some address just one section (e.g. a group programme focusing on 'how to sell') and some (like this book) take clients on the whole journey.

The beauty of it is I can create products and services that I know are addressing my clients' needs and package them up differently to meet different needs, value and time commitment levels.

Putting it all together

We've already covered a lot of ground so far in this book, and hopefully you have already found it valuable and it's helped you learn a lot about yourself. However, some of you may be thinking that this is all well and good, BUT how does this help me with selling?

My answer is that, as with anything worthwhile, we have to start with the right foundations. So, before we move on to **Sell It**, I want to end this section by making sure we understand the importance of the **Live It** and **Love It** steps we have taken and of taking all three steps in order.

We could not begin with **Sell It** without first understanding how life skills are sales skills and how selling does not, and should not, have to be scripted, processed and unnatural.

We started with **Live It** where we addressed our own mindset and how we felt about sales. We thought about why we felt that way, asking what was stopping us and what gets in our way and why. We saw how we can approach things in a different way in order to be fit to travel on this sales journey.

I have worked with clients who have been stopped in their tracks because they were so worried about what people would think. It is a very common problem and you may well be reading this and it completely resonates with you. Let's think about the reality of it, though. How much does a person (usually someone you don't even see that often, like an ex-colleague, or maybe you don't even know them) matter to you personally, and even IF they thought what you were doing was not great, how would it affect your business? Well, it wouldn't. And why? Because the ideal client is the only person you need to worry about, if you want to worry at all.

If you know who this ideal client is, and you know your core values and theirs, they will match. If you understand what their pain is and what their why is, and you take them on the sales road trip, then there will be no judging. Judging is a word that is associated with someone who doesn't see your value, someone who perhaps would like to be like you, but they never can be, and someone who is unlikely to buy from you anyway.

Focus – focus – focus. Lose the fear that will hold you back before you even start to sell. Remember what we said about fear in **Live It** – fear will keep popping up, but we now know what to do with it. (In my case, I've made friends with it!) Look at each part of this book and work through every bit until it feels like driving a car, something which you can do without thinking about it. That is your journey – that is how this all comes together because you will be starting your journey as the true authentic you. Now you are ready for human selling.

Having worked through this section you'll be feeling a lot clearer on:

- your values

- your story

- your ability and personality

- who your ideal client is

- what's troubling them

- where they want to be …and, crucially for your thriving business, how you can help them get there!

So, do you love it? Are you ready to connect with your client?

If you don't feel you are, it may be worth returning to any of the earlier exercises that you feel, being honest with yourself, that you could have engaged with more.

If you are, now you have fallen in love with sales because you have clarity on your why and your passion and now it's time to enjoy the ride. If you are ready to travel, then here we go – we are now going to **Sell It**.

But first... a final exercise before we travel

Just before we start, go and find everything you've noted and created in the exercises so far. You're going to need it for the ride!

Let's make a start on linking it up. Write down a page about who your ideal client is, what they love and what their problems are. This will help you to focus on your ideal client, which will in turn:

- Help you refine your products and services so they match the pain-points of your client

- Help you position these and talk about them in a compelling way

- Help you realise your value fully when you know how you can help and why it matters

Sales is all about matching your value to your ideal client's pain or challenge (or their 'hell'). If there is a true match and you really understand their needs, you will find that a sale has a much stronger chance of happening.

Understand your client's world and make it all about your client - NOT YOU!

It's not about you; it's always about your client

SELL IT

Congratulations! You are about to start your journey. You are fit to travel, you have planned your route and now you are able to actually travel. We are on our way!

The Sales Road Trip

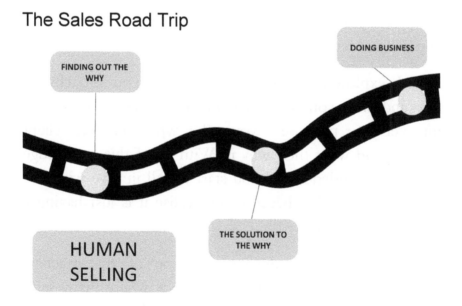

I hope you are feeling that everything is starting to fall into place. The previous chapters have tested you, explained to you why this whole sales process feels the way it does, and given you methods and tips to set all of the elements in place for a smooth journey to your destination – which is where you gain new business.

What could possibly go wrong? Well, there is still time to take a wrong turning, and we all know how frustrating that can be. It can slow you down, you could run out of fuel, and most importantly you may never actually reach your destination. So, it's time to concentrate as the **Sell It** toolkit will fill in all the gaps you may still have. Let's call it your sales satnav – after all you are now travelling on your sales road trip.

It will help you to establish your strategy, and if you do plan on any diversions, you will be in control of those and you will not feel lost.

Live It explored the mindset behind how you sell, why we buy and why you may have blocks. **Love It** started to uncover your purpose – your why, who your ideal client really is and what their why is. With all of this knowledge you gain confidence and you start to fall in love with this process called sales, because you realise it is just having a human conversation.

Now you need to understand some of the practical elements of selling and strategy. This is where many sales coaches would go into tips and tricks to help you become proficient at the sales game. But that's not what the **Live It**, **Love It**, **Sell It** philosophy is about. We don't want to trick anyone, and we don't need to play games. Instead, we'll remind ourselves of the approaches that we all use in our lives every day and see how these equip us beautifully to build relationships and make sales, just by being us. Life skills are sales skills, remember!

Chapter 7

Get Visible

Sell It is all about how you now go out into the world. It is about being visible in the places where your ideal clients are hanging out. It's about telling your story in the right places for the right reasons. Some people get really confused when I say tell your story but it's not about you, it's about the client. That's because it's your story that will connect you to the client and so it *will* be about the client. It will resonate with them, it will make sense, they will trust you and in turn they will see that you have the solution. The themes running through this book can help you to keep a sense-check and ensure you are selling in a human way and in a heart-centred way. In **Sell It** the three key questions we ask (and you should always ask yourself) are: Am I visible? Am I curious? Am I helping?

The storytelling part of **Love It** is now going to be put to use in **Sell It**.

Telling your story

Storytelling is one of the most powerful tools you have in this whole sales road trip. Your story tells you what you are really good at. It informs your mindset (**Live It**). It helps you understand your strengths and your core values (**Love It**). Now in **Sell It** we bring these stories to life for our clients.

We give our stories to our clients because now your story is all about your client. There is a huge connection made through stories. People can relate and they will hear and feel familiarity through stories. When we truly connect and trust someone we are then ready to buy from them, as long as we see value. And value can be shown again through stories. How did our previous clients find working with us? What results and outcomes did they get? Therein is a story.

When you use examples, and especially when they demonstrate a situation much like your client's challenge, they are one of your finest tools to build trust and show you are fully qualified to bring your client the correct solution they need.

Let's just look in more detail at the ways we can use storytelling to enhance our ability to connect in order to sell.

To show that you have walked the walk

Use your own experiences to show that you have walked the walk, that you have experienced exactly what your client has, that you have been in the place where they are now and know how it truly felt. If you don't have direct personal experience of where they are now, it may be you have enough indirect experience to nevertheless understand their situation. For example, I had a client who was a divorce coach who had never been married! Sounds strange, I know! However, she had been a family divorce lawyer in a very high-profile career and she knew everything about divorce that you needed to know. Her experience enabled her to show empathy.

Because of our experiences, we are able to talk honestly about how we overcame problems and found solutions that took us on to the next stage of our journey. We are able to show outcomes using genuine experience and integrity. We can show clients that there is another way and they will realise that we are the ones to help them. The very best way that we can build trust is right here in sharing our story.

Case studies

There is nothing better than a story that involves someone who has worked with you and been through a transformation. It is real and it shows that the work you do is valuable and works. With a case study, you get to tell exactly what the journey looked like because the beauty here is in the detail. It's a step by step account of where you started with the client and what happened to get you to the solution. Having a few of these focused on different scenarios can be very powerful too. Remember to present them in the form of: here's where we started, here's what we did to get the transformation or the results, and this is where the client is today.

Testimonials

Here is another great form of storytelling for **Sell It**. This is the client's story about working with you in their own words. Today we don't just have them in written format; we are now enjoying video testimonials, which are great as they really bring the emotions to life in what the client is saying.

Generic stories

You can also include stories that aren't from your direct experience, stories that are already out there, world stories, stories in the news etc. These can be a very useful addition to your dialogue and for proposals if they fit well. TED Talks are a great source to refer to. TED (www.ted.com) is a non-profit organisation that describes itself as 'devoted to spreading ideas, usually in the form of short, powerful talks'. In TED Talks you can watch and listen to experts sharing their knowledge. I am a great fan of Simon Sinek and I will always talk about his book *Start with Why* and his TED Talk about 'The Golden Circle'. This is priceless storytelling as it then confirms that what you are proposing and recommending is actually out there being used by the experts.

Stories are more powerful than statistics

There is a statistic I came across a couple of years ago:

> *63% of clients remember stories.*
> *Only 5% remember statistics.*

[Source: Dan & Chip Heath]

Ironically, I'm using a statistic to make this point, but the point is that, actually in life as well as in sales, stories carry greater impact than any statistics will. Therefore, use storytelling rather than statistics. It's far more powerful.

When you use story examples, and especially when they demonstrate a situation much like your client's challenge, they are one of your finest tools to build trust and show you are fully qualified to bring your client the correct solution they need.

The importance of getting visible

So why is getting visible so important? The obvious answer is because if people can't see you they won't know about you. Yes, it's that simple. By doing the work on your ideal client you have identified where they hang out. You will also have a good understanding of the language they respond to and what their heaven and hell are. (Check back to **Love It** if you're not sure.)

With this in mind, you now know what to say to these ideal clients and how to connect with them. When you build an audience you are simply connecting. To do this you must be visible. I would cry myself to sleep at night if I thought you'd done all the mindset and research work of **Live It** and **Love It** then not let anyone see who you are! So, let's look at exactly what being visible really looks like and, also importantly, how to be visible and human, rather than visible and sleazy.

Visibility has become one of those overused words in the entrepreneurial world. Here's what I think it means in simple terms: being yourself in the places that matter to your clients.

Being yourself

You must show up as you, not what you think people want you to be or how your competitors are, tempting as that might be. Your ideal clients will connect with you. They will trust their gut that you are the person who can help them. Why? Because the brain makes decisions emotionally first, remember, and your authenticity will show through.

This is important now more than ever. A world where people can gather so much knowledge themselves before they even make a decision or look for you can feel scary when you're trying to sell. In days gone by – the ancient pre-internet era, which I remember, but some of you will be too young to! – sales people were trained to guide and lead the way with our expert knowledge. An awful lot of selling was us telling people what they needed.

Contrast that with today, where people have so much information at their fingertips that they can do their own research on what they need. So why would they buy from you?

They will buy from you because you are *you* and they know, like and trust you. And this is why being visible in the right way is so important. How can our clients and customers be expected to make an informed decision about who we are and what we're like to do business with if we don't show them?

It's our job to be clear about what we do, and even more than that, why we do it. As we saw in **Love It**, connecting with our own why is very powerful. It fires us up, and in turn it fires our ideal clients up too. As entrepreneurs, we have a huge role to play to stay visible and ensure that people know exactly who we are and what we do, but most importantly, why we do it.

Be where they are

So, how do you reach your wonderful prospective clients and customers? The key is to show up in their worlds as much as possible, consistently with the same clear message. Here are the main channels you can use:

Social media platforms

You should have a profile on as many as are relevant to your ideal client. If you're struggling with identifying these, use the tips in **Love It** to deepen your research. Don't try to make this all perfect – remember who you are, your why and storytelling. Link your stories, all of them, to the clients you are talking to. Mix it up. Use some text, some visuals, pictures, video, and also show your behind the scenes and everyday stories too – people love that – it shows you're human. More and more now video is king and I understand this. It is the nearest thing to me actually being with you in the flesh. I can see you, hear the tone of your voice. It even makes sense to think I can make eye contact with you, even if this is one way because you won't necessarily know who is watching, but I'll get that experience as the viewer, that you are talking to me – it doesn't get much better than that virtually! So, get over the fear and just jump on a video and chat! Trust me, when I watch my early videos I do find them a little bit strange, but I am so me now when I do them that it feels great. What you see is what you get, and trust me that is what people want. A great place to start is with short five-minute videos on key topics or top tips, and remember to use your Heaven and Hell exercise to help with your content. It's all there!

Your website

This is your virtual shop window. A great website takes work and understanding, so don't worry if you start with a website that then becomes work in progress. Just start with something to show you exist! Again, you can use all of the work we have done so far to think about how you populate your website with content.

Blogging

Your blog can sit on your website as well as other platforms, and you can also submit your writing as guest blogs to websites with huge followings. Don't forget that content in your blogs is perfect to repurpose on all of your other media, including social media, podcasts and even offline storytelling, speaking and networking for example.

Podcasting

Podcasts are a great way to reach people who like to listen rather than read! Getting your message on a podcast will help you share your knowledge with your audience while they're cooking, in the car, walking the dog etc. Soundcloud is just one brilliant platform to start with, and there are plenty of ways to record audio today with Zoom, iMovie and many more apps that allow you to do this.

Be proactive online

Don't just post on your own profile or page and run. Comment on other posts and answer every comment made on your posts. It's all about having a human conversation. Interaction is key. I always say act online as you would face to face and that will stand you in good stead.

Go offline

Go to events like networking meetings, workshops and exhibitions. There are so many places where you can meet people and network and form new relationships. Learn, speak at workshops and consider running your own if you don't do so already.

Write a book

Books give you credibility like nothing else. They showcase your expertise in one handy package, they help you reach people all over the world, and they open up all sorts of high-profile visibility opportunities. Imagine yourself as an author – how impressive is that? And it's absolutely possible – this book here is the proof! A book can also help you enter the world of public speaking. I speak regularly, and very often get new business from those events. Again, people can see who you are, hear your story and your expertise, and a book backs all of that up.

If reading that list makes you want to lie down, don't worry. You don't have to do it all alone. And you can take it one step at a time. Enlist social media, writing or web design support if you need to – it can make all the difference in you showing up consistently.

And consistency is key. You need to be continually appearing so that people get used to seeing you. How do you get to know the mums or dads at the school gate? You see them every day and you start conversations and get curious. It's exactly the same when you are being visible both online and offline. In the entrepreneurial space there are also opportunities to do reciprocal work. There is every chance that someone needs what you offer as much as you need them. So, let's get together and work together and help each other. Money isn't the only currency available in life.

Choose how often you are going to show up – whether it's through content or in person if you are going offline. This is a critical part of your **Sell It** strategy. No one got anywhere doing something now and again – it takes commitment and dedication to your cause, in this case your why. Don't forget that today you can get many products that help you to schedule posts online, so that can help with the management of this, but again DO NOT post and run. Using such apps is not an excuse for doing nothing else – you have to make showing up to interact part of your daily tasks.

You wouldn't walk through a bar and shove your business card into someone's hand without saying anything, would you? Well if you did, I'm not sure how well you would get on!

So, you know where you're showing up, and you have decided how often it will be. Now here is the really important bit. How are you showing up? What are you going to say? What are you going to tell everyone? How will you attract your ideal client?

Creating your content

This is where the magic happens. Let me explain. This is where everyone gets to know your style, your language, your beliefs, your expertise and your why. This is where you are able to show everyone exactly who you are – your authentic, real true self.

Some may argue that you can't show up online as you would in real life. I accept you may not have the physical and chemical reactions. You may not be able to see body language – unless it's video, of course! – or look someone in the eye, but trust me you can show your authentic self in writing, pictures and particularly in video. Online is much easier than it has ever been to show up as the true you. So, no excuses!

If you're not sure about what to share in your content, think back to the Heaven and Hell exercises you completed in **Love It.** You have identified all the issues and struggles your ideal clients are facing right now. This is a great starting point.

And don't forget to share some of you, too. Content doesn't all have to be sharing what you know. It can also be lessons you're learning along the way, behind the scenes snippets of what it's like in your business, or what's exciting you in your life and work at the moment. All of this lets people in, helps them see the real you and trust you. And, a small amount of posts will be you promoting your amazing products, so don't forget to factor that in.

Exercise

Set yourself a timer for ten minutes and write down all the blog posts, podcast or video topics you can think of.

Chapter 8

Get Curious

So, you've thought about getting out there and being visible. You've thought about where to be and what you can share. This is great for developing the magic triangle of being known, liked and trusted. But what about when you actually meet up with someone, or have a call with them? How can you keep that trust flowing?

The discovery call or meeting is one of the most important parts of this road trip. Here is your chance to get curious and really understand how you can actually help this person. I want to make this the most natural and enjoyable part of the sale, because it can be. However, I appreciate you might find the prospect daunting, and you may be worrying about what the hell it is you need to do now. That is why throughout this whole book I have kept the focus simple. What's your why, who is your ideal client and what is their why? These three things alone will give you all the confidence you need to go into a discovery session. As I say to clients again and again, it's like having a coffee with a friend.

What you do need to consider is this: What is the outcome you want from the discovery call/meeting? It may be you want to send a proposal. It may be that you want to have a second meeting with another decision maker or partner. It may be that you want to put them in touch with someone you are currently working with to chat further about how you can help. Ultimately the outcome you want is a continuation of this relationship – the next stage of working together, and this will be different for every client. All you need to do is think, 'What do I want to know about this person in order to get the outcome that is right for both of us?'

A great reference to help you with this call/meeting is the Heaven and Hell section of **Love It** and also the value journey. With these, you have all the pain in front of you of your ideal client and you know what your product range is in order to get them to heaven. The gaps are getting to know the client, because we can never assume. So, clarification of where they are now is key.

All the information that follows will help you to be confident about this part of the sales journey. I'm going to talk about the key areas to be aware of.

In traditional sales training they talk a lot about 'rapport'. However, 'rapport experts' are then apt to focus on elements such as body language, eye contact and tone of voice. These are, of course, important, but focusing on them is not the way I recommend thinking about rapport.

Take body language. Body language is the non-verbal way that we can communicate with each other. It's said that whereas we can hide the truth in words, our gestures will always tell the truth. The limbic system of the brain controls our non-verbal reactions. Blood will flow to our lips and our pupils will dilate when we see someone attractive or who we love. The jaw position will lower and our eyes will narrow when we receive bad news. We often rub the back of our neck when we feel frustrated or unsure about something. There are also many more signs that can tell us a whole lot about how a person is really feeling.

However, to become an expert at reading body language takes time and experience and we can get it wrong. For example, I

Googled folded arms relating to body language and found the following:

> *The **arms crossed** on chest gesture is universal and is decoded with the same defensive or negative **meaning** almost everywhere. It is commonly seen among strangers in public meetings, in queues or restaurant lines, elevators or anywhere that people feel uncertain or insecure.*

(westsidetoastmasters.com/resources/book_of_body_langua ge/chap4.html)

But what if I'm just cold, and that's the reason I have my arms folded?!

Reading body language and becoming adept at communicating with your own body language might be helpful, and it's something you can choose to spend some time on if you like, but I think it's far more important to focus your attention on building a genuine connection than worrying about what your arms should be doing!

So, what does building rapport mean in the **Live It**, **Love It**, **Sell It** world? It simply means allowing yourself to build a connection. Not letting the gremlins in your head get in the way.

So, rather than thinking about meeting a prospective client for the first time, imagine you're meeting a new friend for coffee. Think back to **Live It** where we talked about life skills being sales skills. There are a whole lot of life skills coming up now!

Maybe a mutual friend has said, 'Oh, you must speak to Jane. You'd get on like a house on fire!' Think about how you'd approach that situation. You would want to find out everything you can about them – fact! We are human and nosey! You will also want them to be interested in you and you will almost certainly want them to like you.

The main skill you will use for this meeting with your new friend will be building rapport! Who knew?

Interestingly, you won't particularly plan this in fine detail. You will trust your instincts and see where the meeting takes you. It's the best way, trust me! I can say that now as we have been engaged together through this book for more than a hundred pages!

You will naturally ask each other questions to build rapport. We form questions on the basis that we know what we want to find out next. Clever, aren't we?

Exactly the same principles apply when we are selling. In order to build rapport, we have to step inside the client's world and be interested in it. I don't mean this flippantly either; I mean really step in and imagine what the world looks like to them. Their world will be different to ours. The things we think are great may not be of interest to them. The way they see colours, interpret words, hear music and see benefits will ALL be different. It is not good enough to assume that they will want to engage with you or buy from you for the same reasons as you think.

This is what I mean by stepping inside their world. It's intense. So rather than give you techniques to clutter your head, I simply invite you to do one thing.

Become curious.

Curiosity isn't a technique – it's an approach to life. (Life skills are sales skills, remember!) People respond to genuine, non-judgemental attention.

How curious are you?

The exercise below is a really interesting one to do with work colleagues and friends. How much do we really know about each other and how much do we assume? You may remember the TV programme *Mr & Mrs*. I remember the original one, but it was revived from 2008 with Phillip Schofield hosting this time, and with celebrities to boot.

It was fascinating how couples who had been married even for over 30 years didn't know the simplest things about each other. Often, this is because we don't stop to ask. Rather than get curious, we assume.

Exercise – Assumptions and how wrong they can be!

This exercise is basically the same as *Mr & Mrs* but without the people being married couples. Put people into pairs – they could be work colleagues or friends or not even know each other. If they don't know each other at all, it definitely makes it interesting because then it becomes all about assumption. Then set one person questions about the other to answer, writing their answers down in silence. That bit is so important. No verbal communication allowed! Questions like:

What car does this person drive?

What car would this person drive if they could drive anything?

What is their favourite food?

What is their favourite music?

Where do they go on holiday?

> *How confident are they on a scale of 1-10, 1 being not confident, 10 being very confident?*
>
> Then compare the results with the person's actual answers. Were you surprised? It's fascinating to see how much we don't really know about other people and how much we assume.

We assume so much about people from how they dress, how they speak and, interestingly, from their body language too. If you want to sell with integrity and then benefit hugely from the ripple effect of referral business and repeat business from long-standing relationships with your clients, NEVER assume anything – just ask. Cultivate a friendly curiosity.

Which leads me nicely on to those magical things called questions.

Questioning

If we are curious, we naturally ask questions. Picture a three-year-old and how many questions they have about the world! They want to find out. They're interested in learning about this wonderful planet, their communities and families. And if you don't ask, you don't learn.

Let's look at the two types of questions we can use. They are simply called open and closed questions. Open questions can never be answered with a YES or a NO. For that reason, they are our knowledge gathering questions. If we want detail, we use open questions. A fun way to remember how they are formulated is 'Five bare bums on a rugby post'!

Five Bare Bums on a Rugby Post

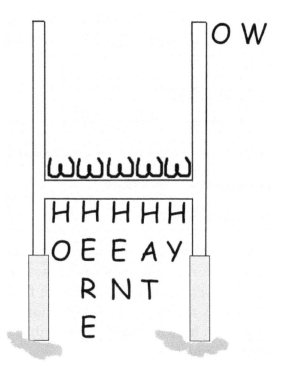

Image by @SteveFoxAST based on @AlanPeat's concept

Who, Where, When, What, Why and How. When you form a question using these words you cannot answer them with Yes or No. As if by magic!

Closed questions can always be answered with Yes and No, but they do have a place too and can help you to clarify that you've understood. Let's go back to meeting your new friend in the coffee shop. Imagine she's just told you a bit about her work, and you want to check you've got it right. You'd say something like, 'So you're a trapeze artist Monday to Thursday and spend Fridays volunteering at the dog shelter, is that right?' You can do the same with your clients. It shows them you have listened and that you do indeed understand what they have said.

Here are some questions you might use with your potential clients, but obviously use them in your own way with your own words:

So, am I right in saying that you…?

You mentioned that you are… is that right?

When I talked about this… that was the idea you liked, wasn't it?

Are you happy to add this… to our goals?

Does that make sense to you?

A client will know how interested you are by the questions you ask and then by the next question you ask when you have listened to their answer. They will recognise a flow that makes sense to them. If they say to you 'good question', then you are awesome because you have officially connected and made them think deeper about something.

So, the other half of the magic formula of great questions is listening. Let's talk about that.

Listening

Just as important as the questions you ask is the way you listen. There's no point creating a fantastic question if you're not going to listen to what the client is actually saying. Listening is quite a complex thing as it involves staying in the moment rather than projecting forward. True active listening takes a fair amount of concentration.

We commonly find ourselves so worried about our next question that we don't listen to the answer we're being given.

So, how can we make sure that we get the maximum out of every interaction we have with our clients?

Like most things in life, it's about practice. The more you do it the better you get. It's all about tuning in. You have to clear out all of the noise around you and concentrate only on that conversation. And, trust me, the noise can also be your own noise: thoughts like, *What are we having for dinner tonight? How will the kids get home?* Even *How am I going to respond to what they are saying?* is unhelpful mental chatter that stops us from truly listening.

Exercise

This is another exercise that I do at workshops and one that I'd like you to try too. You will need at least one other person to do this exercise with.

I put people into pairs. Person A is then asked to talk to Person B for three minutes about any subject they like. It is important that this is strictly timed. During the three minutes that Person A is speaking Person B is not allowed to speak or ask questions. This is really hard to do! Then Person B has two minutes, again strictly timed, to say what they heard.

If you don't tune in properly, you will miss vital information that will stop you being able to talk about what they had said. Please do make sure you do this exercise and put yourself in the Person B role at least once. You can do it with your children, partner, parents, friends or anybody; just get them to talk about anything, but tune in and give it all you've got. The brain is amazing and you will hear so much more than you would have thought when you focus on what's being said rather than what's in your head.

Imagine how many pieces of information you receive every minute of every day.

There was a study conducted by researchers at the University of California, San Diego, under Roger Bohn, and they found that every day people are inundated with the equivalent amount of 34 GB (gigabytes) of information, a sufficient quantity to overload a laptop within a week.

Through mobile phones, the internet, email, television, radio, newspapers, books etc. people receive around 105,000 words every day or 23 words per second of our waking day. Although people can't really read these 105,000 words, this is the real number estimated to be reaching the human eyes and ears every day. After adding pictures, videos, games, etc., we reach the volume of 34 gigabytes of information per day on average.

There are specific neurons that help our brain to filter only things that we are interested in, and so generally we don't reach the point where we're overwhelmed and shut down. All this is even more reason why you have to understand your ideal client and step inside their world. You are able to decide that you are interested in their world, and when you do your brain will help you to filter only the information that is important. It's all about focus, and you can decide how well you are going to listen. Fascinating stuff eh!

Here's an exercise to improve your listening skills – let's call it your auditory workout. Practice makes perfect!

Exercise

Spend some time actively engaged with podcasts, audio books or videos, and when watching and listening make notes of key points mentioned. When you focus you'll be amazed how much you hear and also what you pick up on as the key points.

Mindful listening

Although it's a topic beyond the scope of this book, I find practising mindfulness useful. It helps you to shut out the world and focus.

My friend and mindfulness expert Karen Ramsay-Smith has, though, given me a wonderful exercise to share with you here.

Karen is a Transformational Coach and Mindfulness Guide. She supports women to connect with their truth and soul message, empowering them to feel the freedom and inner strength to come back to a life of love, purpose and fulfilment. Please do look her up, she is wonderful at what she does.

These days we are so focused on our thoughts and actions that we often forget how to listen with care. Practising mindful listening simply means that you are intentionally engaging in the skill of deep listening. The art of listening is as much about your mindset as it is about the actual practice of listening.

This is not something that many of us will have been taught to do in our lives or work! However, when you believe that listening deeply is important and that the practice of listening will bring about positive response, change or action, then this skill will become a great asset to you.

Karen's exercise below is a great way to start practising deep mindful listening.

Exercise – from Karen Ramsay-Smith

This is something that you can use regularly to practise your listening skills.

Choose ten minutes during which you are going to practise mindful listening. At first try this on your own in different surroundings, then later try it with a partner and then as part of a group of people.

1.   Pay attention to your intention

Set your intention to mindful listening. By setting an intention to practise deep listening you have focused your attention on the exercise. You must believe that listening is important, so focus on why you might want to listen more deeply for these ten minutes ahead. Make the commitment to yourself to do this for the full ten minutes.

2.   Remove distractions and get comfy

Turn your phone, laptop, TV or whatever might distract you off or to silent. This will produce the right conditions for mindful listening. Make sure you are comfortable. If you are practising with another person, is there anything that can be done to make them more comfortable and remove distractions for them too?

3.   It's not about YOU

Take the focus away from yourself. Put yourself into the situation fully, the atmosphere or the other person's shoes if you are practising with a partner or group. Practise respect for the experience, situation or other person. If you are thinking about yourself, you won't have the space or attention to give to mindful listening.

4.   Be quiet

We don't often get a chance to practise being quiet in our busy lives, but you need to learn to become still in order to be able to hear the whole experience. If you are not used to being quiet or spending time listening, try a walk outside in nature. Listening in intently to the sound of our natural world can be incredibly calming, healing and will help fine tune your listening skills. Practise trying to listen in for the gaps in any noise of the birds singing, the wind whistling or the rain drops falling.

5.   Be curious

Never make assumptions or assume you know everything. Listen without judgement or the compulsion to react. This is especially important if you are practising mindful listening with another person or group. Making assumptions can make us miss important details in another's response. If you are listening alone while you are in a park for example, then listen more deeply than you normally would. What can you hear that you wouldn't normally hear? How can you listen more intently? Be curious about what is there.

6.   Be kind to yourself and others

You may find that you feel it difficult not to want to start thinking about what YOU want to say next, to butt in or be judgemental in your mind before the other person has finished their sentence. Be patient with yourself and bring yourself back to your original intention – to mindfully listen deeply to this experience and/or the person present. By practising bringing yourself back to the mindful present feeling you will slowly improve your skill. If you found yourself distracted by your own thoughts and you think you may have missed something, you could clarify and ask them if what you think you have heard is correct.

7. Use your heart to listen

Try your best to connect deeply with the experience or the other person. How can you open yourself up more to listening deeper? Allow your heart to listen, so you connect to them on a deeper level than normal. Listening with your heart means practising empathy. When we pause and give empathy and respect we are fully acknowledging that person by holding the space for them to speak. We are allowing the space for unsaid communication to begin. We are allowing the other person to be open towards us, and in turn a sense of awareness of the experience or the other person will become clearer to you.

Want to go deeper? It all starts with you.

The key to cultivating deep mindful listening and genuine connection to others begins with the relationship that we have with ourselves. Practise intentionally and quietly listening to yourself and your own heart so that you may notice the thoughts, feelings and sensations that arise in yourself. Rather than trying to put them to one side, just be aware of their presence.

If you take time out to listen in and understand yourself more with empathy, love and non-judgement, you will begin to feel more appreciation and compassion for yourself. This in turn will help you to feel more respectful, loving and compassionate for others and will improve your genuine connection, your deep listening skills and improve your relationship with yourself and others.

'Listen and attend with the ear of your heart.'
St Benedict

Chapter 9

Get Helping

Having used all of these wonderful life skills such as questioning, listening and really getting curious, it's time to go on to the next part of the journey. You have all the answers to the questions and you are sure of your client's why. Remember when you have done the discovery call or meeting you will have had a goal. This could be to gain a second meeting or maybe to actually put a proposal together so it confirms and clarifies everything you have discussed. I will show you some great proposal tips in this chapter, but first you have to bring your call or meeting to a close. This is where sometimes you hear the phrase 'close the sale'. This is where the pressure starts to build, and it can become quite stressful. Often my clients tell me that they don't know what to do here. They've had a great chat, but they don't know what to do now.

So, think again of it as a meeting with a new friend who you have met for the first time. I like to take you back to comfortable scenarios because this is where you will act more like the true you. When you've had your coffee and chat do you just stand up and say goodbye and walk away? Probably not, well unless you really didn't like each other! But you did like this new friend because you want to see them again, or certainly speak again, either to find out a bit more and progress your relationship further or to build a long-term relationship. In this case the relationship is the sale, and that's just how I like to think of a sale. The saying goes, 'We don't make a sale; we make a relationship.'

For those reasons, we will make an arrangement for the next step: a date for a next meeting or a proposal to outline the ways you can have that relationship.

So, here are just a couple of sentences that will help you to take control of the end of the meeting or call. Firstly:

'I can definitely help you.'

This sentence is a gem and demonstrates that you understand the client's challenge and you have the expertise to give them the outcome they desire. The word 'help' is a great word to use as it is very empathetic. Add to that the confident nature of the statement and it will help the client feel like they trust you and they are at ease with you. It's a relief that you can help. Follow this with:

'What I'm going to do for you is…'

This phrase has to feel like your language and has to be said naturally, so use your own words. But what this type of opening does psychologically is put you firmly in control of what happens next – after all, you are the expert! The other joy of this phrase is it shows you are doing something for them, which again builds trust and empathy. You are all about helping them. It's all about the client.

Whatever you do next will align with your goal at the start of the call or meeting, which may be a proposal or a further meeting with another stakeholder, for example.

Make a relationship not a sale

If it were up to me I would ban the phrase 'closing the sale'. It has nothing about it that feels good and comfortable. It conjures up pressure and restriction on options and timescales. I would rather say this is the start of the relationship, because that is true – or certainly you hope so. Even if they don't do business with you here and now, it could still be the start of something that will manifest in, say, six months' time. Don't close anything down – keep all lines open.

There are experts who say you should 'close people down' as soon as possible so if you're having a great conversation you should make the offer there and then.

Let me ask you a question, though. Let's say you are organising a charity event with a friend and you have done all the brainstorming of facts and goals. Do you there and then put the event together? I suspect, rather than book the venue, speaker and organise tickets on the spot, you'd go away and think about everything you have talked about and put it into a comprehensive plan.

As entrepreneurs, I suggest we do a similar thing with our clients. There are a couple of things that can happen when you do it this way. The client will very likely feel like you are actually going to take some time to consider what they really need. The other thing that happens is that you have time to ensure the solution you suggest is right for the client. A great proposal will have a great impact.

The proposal

A great way to get to the next stage is to prepare a proposal for your client. The mention of the word proposal will trigger various emotions for some people. If you have been in corporate sales like I have, you may visualise a 20-plus page document that is time consuming and complex, and when you don't get the deal feels like such a waste of time! Or perhaps you have never prepared a proposal at all and are not sure where to even start.

Here's a top tip which really helps to maintain the connection you have started to build and make life really easy. **Ask the client what they would like to see in the proposal.** That way they are building their own proposal and you will see what things they feel are important to see in that proposal. There is nothing worse than sending the above-mentioned 20-plus pages of proposal containing things they are just not interested in. And remember a proposal is not about you, so don't start it with all about your background, your testimonials and you. A proposal should be all about making it clear that you understand the client and what you are going to do for them to get them the outcome you know they desire, because you have spent time finding out – you didn't assume. If you want to add links for testimonials and social media profiles then do so, but right at the end – make that the icing on the cake.

If you are very experienced and you have a very clear view of what they need from you, or maybe your solution is a simple one, then feel free to outline in words what you are going to do for them whilst you are still with them on the call or face to face. It's almost a teaser when you talk about the solution and you will build excitement if you have built rapport.

Never forget the golden rule if you are going to talk about solutions – make sure you time it right. If you offer the solution too soon, and you haven't built rapport or even uncovered the client's why, you are in danger of looking like you're not listening and you could risk appearing pushy.

When I worked at Yellow Pages most of my clients were people who already had adverts in the Yellow Pages book. Our strategy was fact find on the first call and on the second call present proposal and close. Very corporate language, I know, but to put that into our human language it was two conversations, with the first being about listening. This allowed me time to get some draft adverts done and put some pricing together with the reasons why and what the potential outcomes would be for the client. I couldn't possibly have done this in one call.

Take time over your client. They are going to invest in you as their expert, so show them that you *are* an expert. Make the sale considered from your side, which will make it feel that same way for the client.

Don't rush. Be considerate, build rapport and make sure you absolutely understand exactly why your client wants to buy – that is the only way you can match your solution in a heart-centred and genuine way. Trust me, this will make so much difference to forging these great relationships you will have. And always remember the ripple effect. Everything you do from the minute you meet a client will have an impact. Some clients will make quick decisions and once in a while you will get that dream client that says, 'So what happens next. How do I work with you?' It really does happen, but the usual experience is that it can take a little longer than that depending on what you are selling.

So, let's assume you're meeting your client for the first time and you're *not* going to ask for the sale at your first meeting. It could be a face-to-face meeting or held over a video link. It doesn't matter; the principle is the same. Here's how to go about sharing your solution with your client instead – and this way it feels human, not sleazy.

At the end of the first meeting with your client you will tell them something like, 'What I am going to do for you is…' and then explain that you will prepare a proposal showing the solution you recommend for them, by a certain date and with the information in it that they want to see. (You won't forget the proposal tip above, so you will have already asked them about what they want to see in it, and when it comes to write the proposal you will, of course, include those elements.) At the same time book in a new meeting or call so that you can discuss the proposal with them once they have had time to digest it. This keeps the momentum going. If they don't want to book in a firm appointment, just suggest that you will give them a call in a week's time. They then know that you will want to know the outcome. That's perfectly ok. You have spent time with them and you will want to see if that time was productive.

Make that follow-up call based on when the client feels they will have time to look at the proposal. Here is another way for you to gauge interest, from how keen they are to give time to this. I would say seven days maximum is a good time to be talking again, so aim to get the next call or meeting into that timescale, but let the client feel they are driving that from their side.

So, use questions like:

How soon do you think you will look at the proposal?

How soon do you want to start work on this?

These will help you to see what their timescales are, and of course how serious they are about working with you and solving their problem or challenge.

Use phrases like:

I want to give you time to consider everything, and then we can get back together to discuss.

Phrases like this show respect and don't pressure or smother them, but nevertheless set expectations that you want to talk again.

Sending the proposal

Whatever you do, send the proposal when you said you would send it – no later! Not sticking to your word and being late here can lose the sale. I recommend you make the proposal a two-to-three-page PDF document. Using a PDF looks more professional than using a Word document. (Also, it can't be so easily changed. I've even seen it happen where a price sent to a client was changed by a them! Yep, it's a tough world out there so just cross your 't's and dot your 'i's.) Keeping it to two to three pages should help you keep it simple and focused. You just need to outline how you'd like to help them and what they can expect from you, making sure you include everything you have been asked to and promised to include. The document will then give the client an opportunity to read through it for themselves without feeling overwhelmed with information or cornered.

To give you a framework, here are the headings from my simple proposal document that you can consider using, building in what the client has asked to see within these headings.

Always remember the proposal is all about the client.

Your objective/goals – I.e. the client's objective/goals. This makes it clear that you have listened and understood their goals.

My focus and responsibilities for you are as follows – This is your accountability to your client.

As an outcome of the work I will do with you, you will have the following in place... – These are the client's outcomes. Only ever make promises that you know you can keep.

How I will work with you – Here you set the boundaries and manage expectations, providing details of the journey they will go on whilst working with you.

My time and value to you – Here you match your why to their why and also manage expectations on timescales and working hours etc.

Your investment – This is the money, but by positioning it like this it feels more like you are talking about value. You can also detail the order of the services in the proposal here.

Why I can help – Here you can refer to testimonials, case studies etc. You do this right at the end because: it's not about you; it's about the client. But this just shows that you are credible as the expert to provide the right solution and outcome for them.

And here's an example of a proposal written using those headings. This is a fictitious proposal, but one based on the kind of services my business provides in reality.

Proposal for ABC Company Ltd - 12th June 20XX

Your objective/goals

- To coach the team and individual salespeople to achieve performance results and not miss opportunities

- Review and refine strategy and enable creative thinking when it comes to sales, as well as accountability

- Create individual strategy plans to achieve the targets they have submitted

- Continue to build, inclusively, on the great team that you already have in place

My focus and responsibilities for you are as follows:

- Engage with all staff to coach and enhance their sales skills in order to increase company revenue

- Feedback regularly to you, Emma, from the team and individual coaching sessions

- Align company and team objectives to the content of every session and workshop

- Empower staff to make and achieve their own goals and sustain the sales effort

As an outcome of the work I will do with you, you will have the following in place:

- Accountability from sales people to keep their own consistency and motivation

- Key goals set for all staff – both through 1-2-1 coaching and team workshops

- Positivity and focus in their daily work

- Engaged and energised team

- Increased sales!

How I would work with you

- Before workshops and coaching would start I would meet with you to make some firm goals for what we would like to achieve, and these will be our working goals as we progress.

- I like to work as part of the team and not as a complete outsider coming in to tell them what to do!

- Our starting date for the monthly workshops and 1-2-1 coaching would need to be agreed, and as discussed I would suggest we consider w/c 30th July to start the workshops, with 1-2-1 coaching on a fortnightly basis from August, leading in to October starting dates for your Heads.

My time and value

With my service to you, Emma, I will be available on an app called Voxer for you if you need to chat through anything. I would respond to anything between the hours of 9-5pm Mon - Fri and always within 24 hrs, unless I am on holiday which I will give prior notice of to you. In the coming period I have a week at the end of August planned, but nothing else. The two individuals who will have 1-2-1 coaching will also have access.

My productivity and results will be reliant on full participation from the team and the Management team also. I will have regular catch ups to talk through progress with the Management. Emma, please think about how often you will want to catch up.

Your Investment

Based on our conversation, I have quoted for a programme of workshops for 6 months and 1-2-1 coaching for your two new Heads of Department. This coaching would be beneficial on a fortnightly basis from August through to October and then we can review and decide on any further work.

Working on this basis allows me to have consistency with the sales team over a period of time and bond as part of the team. It is important that I gain trust and that the team buy into me as someone who will support and mentor them in their daily job. I am friend not foe. That will get us the best results.

I would also look to meet with you to create the goals mentioned above. My costs include the meetings that you and I will have, Emma – I don't charge extra for those, and you can let me know whether a monthly catch up is good for you or whether you would like something more often.

I also will send SurveyMonkey questionnaires after all of the workshops, so we can continue to get feedback, review and refine where necessary for the team. These are their workshops and I want them to own them.

All travel costs, preparation and meetings with you are included in my quote.

Workshop 6 x 1 per month @ £xxx per workshop	£xxxx
1-2-1 coaching @ £xxx an hour - 12 hour sessions	£xxx
Total for 6 months work	£xxxx
Monthly total due 1st month	£xxxx

My payment terms are 7 days from date of invoice. No VAT is applicable for this proposal.

Why I can help

More about my bio is available on LinkedIn:
www.linkedin.com/in/juleswhite134

Also for any testimonials you can look at my website:
www.liveitloveitsellit.co.uk

I also have a Facebook business page where you will see more about my work and recommendations:
www.facebook.com/liveitloveitsellit

My podcast is also here if you would like a listen:
goo.gl/e4xxQS

If this becomes a successful working arrangement for both parties, I would be delighted to continue work beyond the 6 months.

I hope this all makes sense and if you have any questions whatsoever then I will be happy to answer them.

I look forward to the opportunity of working with you.

Kind regards

Jules

Jules White
Live It Love It Sell It

When you have finished writing your proposal check the document thoroughly. Read it back through and use a spellcheck to ensure that it makes sense and contains no mistakes before you hit send.

What next?

Never send a proposal and just wait for a response. You need to know how your client feels about it. And you can always benefit from feedback. Even if your client says no this time, there's valuable learning to be done in listening to them and understanding why this time is not right. So, make sure you follow up with the call or meeting you agreed at your first meeting. Then use your questioning and listening skills to understand what they thought of your proposed solutions. If they didn't see value, find out why. What did you miss? How could it be better next time?

If you can't get hold of them once it's sent or they cancel the meeting you had arranged, you should never make assumptions about why that is. I have had clients who had an issue arise in their lives and so the timing was no longer right for them, but they came back later on and we worked together, probably because I stayed in touch without being pushy and just checked in with them.

Pricing and negotiation

A question I sometimes get asked when it comes to proposals is whether you should quote a total inclusive price or give the client a shopping list type of price list, breaking all the elements down.

My answer is either. However, if the price is fully inclusive, then ensure that somewhere you explain what you get for the price. They need to see value.

The thing to bear in mind is this: when you are making a recommendation you are making it based on giving the client the right solution, so however you break your pricing down the proposal is your expert recommendation of what will be their best solution.

There is also the possibility of giving them two or three overall options, a bronze, silver, gold type of offer. As long as if you do this, you are clear about the value and impact that each option will have in solving their challenge or pain. This applies to both service- and product-based offerings.

A positive to offering such a choice is the client is less likely to want to batter you down on price because there are already a couple of ways they can work with you. They already have a choice; and in typical human style we will not usually want the most expensive and we certainly don't feel great about having the cheapest, so your most popular package will very likely be the silver package. Therefore, make sure that is a really good impact package and *voilà*, you have solved a good part of the negotiation process before it even began!

And talking of negotiation, I, of course, want to address that directly. It's definitely a real element of sales, but again it's something that's apt to stir up fears and people can often feel out of their depth or intimidated, and we can panic into immediate submission via a discount! Or as I like to call it 'you drop your pants'! It's a well know sales phrase.

So firstly, if a client wants to negotiate, it may be for a few different reasons. It is not always about price. It may be that part of what you have suggested is something they feel they don't need. So, make sure you understand their reasons for negotiating.

If you follow my thoughts about how to set out the pricing in the proposal – or the part about 'your investment', which I much prefer – you can alleviate a lot of negotiation by doing it this way.

If your client is still adamant they want a 'deal', then here is a lovely piece of magic for you. You can quite confidently say that there is nothing that you could recommend that they take out of what you have suggested. However, if they want to reduce the package, what would they like to take out?

This firmly puts the ball in their court. Whatever they take out now is their responsibility and often they won't want to be the one making that decision. Here you will discover how strong you can be, and not because this is a battle, because actually any sale should be win-win, but if you do fold, or give in or discount, then you may not provide the brilliant outcome or product that you know they need from what they told you. My question to you is: Are you ready to devalue your offering and risk not getting the right results for your client? Remember the ripple effect from you not delivering what they need can be brutal. Sometimes people are very happy to talk about what went wrong ...to everyone.

You will gain far more respect by sticking to your value or even walking away. Sell with integrity, stay true to you and sell with soul.

Sell with empathy

You may come across objections along the way, but I always think objections come from people not understanding what you offer and your value. There is a knowledge gap when we get objections. When you want to disagree with something it can be because you don't understand the other person's point of view, and we have a responsibility to bridge those gaps. I see negotiation as a type of objection because the client wants to change something, and they absolutely have the right to do that.

The big thing to remember when selling is that every day in life you handle objections, whether they are from family, partners, children, friends or colleagues. If you handle them as a battle, you will see them escalate into an argument, which makes the situation much harder to resolve. If you try to understand the objection, you have a much greater chance of reaching an amicable conclusion. You may have to agree to disagree, but it is always possible to get to some sort of agreement.

My advice in sales is sell with empathy, always. Never go into battle. There are always casualties on both sides, and who wants that? Understand why the client has an objection or wants to negotiate and satisfy their needs. Some may say this sounds too wishy-washy and you're giving in. That would be to misunderstand. As sales people we have to take control and we mustn't give in.

Remember what we are doing here. We are making a relationship, NOT making a transaction, and so sell with empathy. The beauty of relationships is they last longer than a single transaction, so by conducting yourself with integrity and empathy rather than focusing on 'winning' you're likely to generate future business. Your client will come back to you when they need you, and they'll recommend you to others. That's the real win.

We have an old sales technique that was always taught in the mundane sales training environments, but some of these tips are still good to know. It's called 'Feel, Felt, Found'. It's all about empathy and relating to the client's concerns or problems.

I understand how you feel,

I felt the same way too,

but what I found was…

This is a perfect example of really knowing how the client feels but helping them realise that there is a solution to their problem and actually you are exactly the person to solve it.

Don't fear objections or negotiation. I haven't made a big deal out of it in this book because there is no need to focus on what might go wrong. Think of it as learning, but never give in, submit and devalue what you have to offer. Sell it with confidence, empathy and integrity. Live it – you are fit to travel the road trip, so own this trip. Make it the trip of a lifetime every time you travel it. Love it, and know that what you have is magic and, most importantly, what you have your client needs.

Sell It is all about going out there with all the knowledge you already have and adding in the magic of **Live It** and **Love It**. The questions to always remember when you are finally on your road trip are:

Am I visible?

Am I being curious?

Am I helping?

If the answers to all of these are a big fat YES, then you have reached your destination. You know that simply by being you, you have something unique to offer. You know how to tap into that and how to leave behind the myths and mindset gremlins that create fear. And you know how to make a genuine connection with your customer. You can now **Sell It**.

There is an onward journey to go on and who knows I may write a book about that where we look at what happens after the sale. In the meantime, let's look at how far we have come and celebrate the amazing journey we have travelled.

So, what could TripAdvisor say about the sales road trip?

On this fantastic road trip we saw that in actual fact our own life skills make us natural born sellers. We had been told a few myths about where we were going, which were quite worrying, but actually when we got there it was very beautiful and very relaxing too, and definitely not scary.

We met fear on the journey and he wasn't as bad as some of the reviews had said he would be because we basically made friends. Nice chap actually – he had our best intentions at heart.

It was definitely a journey of discovery. One of those trips where you grow as a person and find out a lot about yourself, and we would have so much more confidence next time we come back.

We would sum it up as being a trip that everyone should go on. It changed our whole perspective of sales. It was certainly not a destination we had considered going to as it felt a bit sleazy, but when we finally arrived after an enlightening trip it will be a place we revisit forever more.

Thank you for creating such an amazing journey.

A final exercise

How about you? Take some time to reflect on your own journey through this book. What obstacles have you uncovered and overcome? What lightbulbs have switched on for you?

Whenever you wobble (and we all do) think about the power you have within you to help others. I argue that you have a duty to do just that – so get out there with your gifts and **Live It, Love It, Sell It**!

Afterword

This book began its journey in August 2017. It turned out not to be the book I first thought I would write because I'd originally planned to write about my experience in sales and the lead up to my successful pitch in the Dragons' Den where Peter Jones and Theo Paphitis were both bidding to invest in my Truly Madly Baby business, but that day in August I met the amazing Gayle Johnson who was to help and inspire me to create something else instead, something really special to me and, hopefully, to you too. She helped bring **Live It**, **Love It**, **Sell It**, the book and the philosophy, to life. From that day I haven't looked back.

This was a story that really needed to be written because for years I have battled against a picture of sales that was a misrepresentation of what sales can and should be about. Sales isn't or shouldn't be about being pushy, driving numbers and ego-driven clichéd scripts. I knew instinctively that it was about the human connection, relationships and actually loving the relationships we create, because by nature we love helping people. This is sales. Everything you have read was written by me from the heart and from real life experience. And yes, it is my own opinion. Like all salespeople, I won't be able to sell to everyone, nor do I want to. This book is dedicated to the people who are the brave warriors out there making a difference by giving back everything they have learnt and built through their lives with passion and innovation – the entrepreneurs.

I hope you loved the journey we have travelled. I hope you have had many lightbulb moments and I hope you now have an even greater love for your businesses, because you now see that sales is about you sharing your why and connecting with your ideal client's why, and that sales is you and your business.

This book can now be your best friend as you grow and enjoy your business. The entrepreneurs' best friend from the entrepreneurs' sales coach. Let it always guide you and hold your hand. It should have lifetime value that you can always use. The content won't date because it's about human selling. People buy people and people buy people they trust. Always trust that if you are your true self, then you will sell with soul, and what better way is there to sell?

Happy Selling!

I'll leave the last word to my beautiful dad and something he always used to tell me:

'There's no such word as can't.'

About the Author

Jules White is a professional sales coach whose business allows her to do what she loves, helping entrepreneurs and businesses to succeed at sales and to fall in love with selling.

She has over 30 years' experience of business and sales, including winning investment from Peter Jones on the second series of *Dragons' Den* for her business Truly, Madly, Baby, making her a real dragon slayer.

She is a regular public speaker covering sales, business and life subjects. Inspired by the words her beloved late father used to tell her, her 'No such word as can't' talk aims to show everyone they can do whatever they want to do.

Jules also hosts the podcast 'The Human Conversation' on iTunes and Soundcloud.

Live It, Love It, Sell It is her first book.

You can work with Jules on a one-to-one basis, attend one of her workshops or learn through one of her online courses. Details of these and more can be found at:

www.liveitloveitsellit.co.uk